WHERE LIVING THINGS LIVE

McGRAW-HILL
SCIENCE
MACMILLAN/McGRAW-HILL EDITION

WHERE LIVING THINGS LIVE

RICHARD MOYER ■ LUCY DANIEL ■ JAY HACKETT
PRENTICE BAPTISTE ■ PAMELA STRYKER ■ JOANNE VASQUEZ

NATIONAL GEOGRAPHIC SOCIETY

McGraw-Hill School Division
New York   Farmington

Program Authors

Dr. Lucy H. Daniel
Teacher, Consultant
Rutherford County Schools,
North Carolina

Dr. Jay Hackett
Emeritus Professor of Earth
Sciences
University of Northern
Colorado

Dr. Richard H. Moyer
Professor of Science
Education
University of Michigan-
Dearborn

Dr. H. Prentice Baptiste
Professor of Curriculum and
Instruction
New Mexico State
University

Pamela Stryker, M.Ed.
Elementary Educator and
Science Consultant
Eanes Independent School
District
Austin, Texas

JoAnne Vasquez, M.Ed.
Elementary Science
Education Specialist
Mesa Public Schools,
Arizona
NSTA President 1996–1997

NATIONAL GEOGRAPHIC SOCIETY
Washington, D.C.

Contributing Authors

Dr. Thomas Custer
Dr. James Flood
Dr. Diane Lapp
Doug Llewellyn
Dorothy Reid
Dr. Donald M. Silver

Consultants

Dr. Danny J. Ballard
Dr. Carol Baskin
Dr. Bonnie Buratti
Dr. Suellen Cabe
Dr. Shawn Carlson
Dr. Thomas A. Davies
Dr. Marie DiBerardino
Dr. R. E. Duhrkopf
Dr. Ed Geary
Dr. Susan C. Giarratano-Russell
Dr. Karen Kwitter
Dr. Donna Lloyd-Kolkin
Ericka Lochner, RN
Donna Harrell Lubcker
Dr. Dennis L. Nelson
Dr. Fred S. Sack
Dr. Martin VanDyke
Dr. E. Peter Volpe
Dr. Josephine Davis Wallace
Dr. Joe Yelderman

Invitation to Science, *World of Science*, and *FUNtastic Facts* features found in this textbook were designed and developed by the National Geographic Society's Education Division.
Copyright © 2000 National Geographic Society

The name "National Geographic Society" and the Yellow Border Rectangle are trademarks of the Society, and their use, without prior written permission, is strictly prohibited.

Cover Photo: bkgrd. Craig K. Lorenz/Photo Researchers, Inc.; inset, Richard Price/FPG

McGraw-Hill School Division
A Division of The McGraw-Hill Companies

Copyright © 2000 McGraw-Hill School Division,
a Division of the Educational and Professional
Publishing Group of The McGraw-Hill Companies, Inc.

All rights reserved. No part of this book may be reproduced or transmitted in any form or by any means, electronic or mechanical, including photocopying, recording, or by any information storage and retrieval system, without permission in writing from the publisher.

McGraw-Hill School Division
Two Penn Plaza
New York, New York 10121

Printed in the United States of America

ISBN 0-02-278213-3 / 3

1 2 3 4 5 6 7 8 9 058/046 05 04 03 02 01 00 99

CONTENTS

UNIT 6 — WHERE LIVING THINGS LIVE

CHAPTER 11 • GETTING ALONG 321

Topic 1: PLACES TO LIVE 322
- **EXPLORE ACTIVITY** Investigate Where Plants and Animals Live 323
- **SKILL BUILDER** Defining Terms Based on Observations: A Forest Community 328
- **NATIONAL GEOGRAPHIC WORLD OF SCIENCE** Homes on Land and Sea 330

Topic 2: FOOD 332
- **EXPLORE ACTIVITY** Investigate Where Food Comes From 333
- **QUICK LAB** Decomposers 337
- **SCIENCE MAGAZINE** Foods Around the World 340

Topic 3: ROLES FOR LIVING THINGS 342
- **EXPLORE ACTIVITY** Investigate How Living Things Meet Their Needs 343
- **QUICK LAB** Traveling Seeds 348
- **SCIENCE MAGAZINE** People Who Need People 350

CHAPTER 11 REVIEW/PROBLEMS AND PUZZLES 352

CHAPTER 12 • KEEPING IN BALANCE 353

Topic 4: COMPETITION 354
- **EXPLORE ACTIVITY** Investigate How Much Room Plants Need 355
- **QUICK LAB** Musical Chairs 358
- **SCIENCE MAGAZINE** Enough to Go Around 360

Topic 5: FIT FOR SURVIVING 362
- **DESIGN YOUR OWN EXPERIMENT** How Does the Shape of a Bird's Beak Affect What It Eats? 363
- **SKILL BUILDER** Observing: Identifying Properties of an Environment 367
- **SCIENCE MAGAZINE** Leapin' Lizards! 370

Topic 6: THINGS CHANGE 372
- **EXPLORE ACTIVITY** Investigate What Happens When Ecosystems Change 373
- **QUICK LAB** Crowd Control 378
- **SCIENCE MAGAZINE** Too Many Rabbits! 380

CHAPTER 12 REVIEW/PROBLEMS AND PUZZLES 381
UNIT 6 REVIEW/PROBLEMS AND PUZZLES 382–384

REFERENCE SECTION

DIAGRAM BUILDERS
BUILDING A FOOD WEB

HANDBOOK R1
MEASUREMENTS R2–R3
SAFETY R4–R5
COLLECT DATA R6–R10
MAKE MEASUREMENTS R11–R17
MAKE OBSERVATIONS R18–R19
REPRESENT DATA R20–R23
USE TECHNOLOGY R24–R26

GLOSSARY R27
INDEX R39

UNIT 6
WHERE LIVING THINGS LIVE

CHAPTER 11
GETTING ALONG

Wherever you live on Earth, there are many different living things sharing the same space. You also share space with things that are nonliving. What's in your space, besides you?

In Chapter 11 you will find and use different ways to represent information. You can use arrows, labels, and pictures.

Topic 1
LIFE SCIENCE

WHY IT MATTERS

You share your living space with many living and nonliving things.

SCIENCE WORDS

ecosystem all the living and non-living things in an environment

community all the living things in an ecosystem

population all the members of a certain type of living thing in an area

habitat the place where a plant or animal naturally lives and grows

Places to Live

What might happen if a giraffe found itself in a desert? How well do you think it would survive?

Organisms live in special places. A frog lives in a pond. A cactus lives in a desert. A giraffe lives on a savanna. Each place has special things that the organisms need. The pond has water to keep the frog wet. The desert has sunshine to help the cactus grow. What does the savanna provide for the giraffe?

EXPLORE

HYPOTHESIZE Why do organisms live where they do? Write a hypothesis in your *Science Journal*. How might you test your ideas?

EXPLORE ACTIVITY

Investigate Where Plants and Animals Live

Explore why plants and animals live where they do.

PROCEDURES

MATERIALS
- magazines
- scissors
- *Science Journal*

1. Using the magazines and scissors, cut out pictures of 4 different environments. Look for pictures of deserts, forests, ponds, and grasslands. Spread the pictures on a table.

2. **OBSERVE** Cut out 8 pictures of different plants and animals and trade them for the plant and animal pictures cut out by another group. Look at the pictures carefully. To which environment do you think each plant or animal is best suited for survival? Give reasons for your choices.

3. **MAKE DECISIONS** Place the plant and animal pictures under the environment you have chosen for them.

CONCLUDE AND APPLY

1. **IDENTIFY** What are the characteristics of the organisms that live in each environment? Make a list.

GOING FURTHER: Apply

2. **INFER** What determines where organisms live?

Where Do Plants and Animals Live?

The Explore Activity shows that different plants and animals live in different places. However, all plants and animals live in **ecosystems** (ek′ō sis′temz). An ecosystem is made up of all the living and nonliving things in a certain area. What living things might you find in one area? What nonliving things might you find?

An ecosystem can be as small as the space underneath a rock.

The living and nonliving parts of an ecosystem affect each other in different ways. For example, a tree grows in soil. When dead leaves fall from the tree, small organisms in the soil break down the leaves. The leaves now become part of the soil.

What might you see if you looked under a rock? A **community** (kə mū′ni tē) of insects, worms, and fungi! A community is all the living things in an ecosystem.

An ecosystem can be as large as one of the Great Lakes.

Each community can be divided into **populations** (pop′yə lā′shənz). A population is all the members of a single type of organism. For example, you might find a population of pill bugs under a rock.

Each living thing has a **habitat** (hab′i tat′). A habitat is a living thing's home. A frog's habitat is in or near a pond. A centipede's habitat is in the soil under a rock.

What Habitats Are Found in a Pond?

A pond ecosystem has many different habitats. Each habitat meets the needs of the organisms that live there. Living things need food, water, and a place to live. They also need space to grow and reproduce.

All living things in a pond ecosystem depend on other living things. The living part of the ecosystem also depends on the non-living part of the ecosystem.

A POND ECOSYSTEM

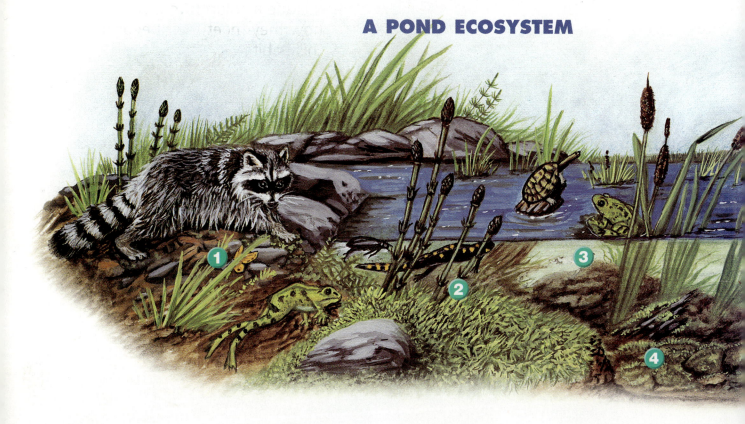

❶ The Banks
Plants like ferns and moss live along pond banks. Animals include insects, mice, snakes, raccoons, and birds.

❷ The Water's Edge
Plants on the water's edge live partly underwater. Animals include salamanders, snails, and water bugs.

❸ Shallow Water
Floating plants live in the shallow water. Frogs sit on top of lily pads and hunt insects. Turtles come up on rocks or logs to lie in the Sun.

❹ Algae
Algae are single-celled or many-celled organisms. A pond may contain billions of algae. You can see algae on rocks and logs in a pond.

Algae depend on sunlight and pond water to survive. Insects and small animals depend on the algae for food. Frogs depend on these insects and other animals for food. Fish depend on frogs and tadpoles for food. The heron depends on both frogs and fish for food. Each organism depends on others. All of the organisms depend on the pond.

READING DIAGRAMS

1. **WRITE** How many different habitats are there in a pond ecosystem? Name each of them.
2. **REPRESENT** Choose three of the living things that live in a pond ecosystem. Make a chart that shows each organism's habitat. Include a column that shows how they meet their needs in this habitat.

5 Deep Water Floating plants live here too. Fish also live in deep water.

6 Great Blue Heron The heron flies to different habitats. It comes to the pond to get its favorite foods — frogs, fish, and tadpoles.

7 Dragonfly Adult dragonflies live out of the water. Young dragonflies are like fish. They live in the water and breathe through gills.

8 Bladderwort Bladderwort is a floating plant. The stems and leaves of the plant have air sacs. When a small organism touches an air sac, it is sucked into the air sac and eaten!

Skill: Defining Terms Based on Observations

A FOREST COMMUNITY

You have learned that a community is all the living things in an ecosystem. Different ecosystems have different communities. For example, the pond community on pages 326 and 327 included bladderwort, frogs, algae, and dragonflies. What makes up a forest community? Look at the picture on this page. Use your observations to define a forest community.

MATERIALS
- *Science Journal*

PROCEDURES

1. **OBSERVE** Look at the illustration of a forest. What do you see? Make a list in your *Science Journal*.

2. **CLASSIFY** Which of the things on your list are living? Which are nonliving?

CONCLUDE AND APPLY

DEFINE Using your lists, define a forest community.

WHY IT MATTERS

Ecosystems, communities, habitats, and populations are part of your own life. You live in an ecosystem. It has living and nonliving parts. You also occupy a habitat in your ecosystem.

Brain Power
What are some living and nonliving things in your ecosystem?

REVIEW

1. What is an ecosystem?
2. What is a community? List some members of a community in a pond ecosystem.
3. How is a community different from a population?
4. **DEFINE** Think about the habitat of a pet dog. List some of its characteristics. Use your list to write your own definition of *habitat*.
5. **CRITICAL THINKING Apply** How would a pond ecosystem change if the water in the pond dried up?

WHY IT MATTERS THINK ABOUT IT
Describe the kinds of living things that share your habitat.

WHY IT MATTERS WRITE ABOUT IT
Of all the living things that share your habitat, which is your favorite? Which is your least favorite? Why?

NATIONAL GEOGRAPHIC World of Science

Homes
on Land and Sea

Caribou are a kind of deer. They live in cold northern regions.

Geography Link

Giant tube worms live at the bottom of the sea.

Where do animals and plants live? Everywhere! Some strange creatures live at the bottom of the sea . . . by underwater volcanoes!

Most life on Earth depends in some way on the Sun, but no sunlight reaches the bottom of the sea. However, boiling water flows out of volcanoes on the ocean floor. The water contains chemicals from deep within the Earth.

Unusual bacteria use these chemicals instead of sunlight to make their own food. Many other living things depend on the bacteria, including giant tube worms. The worms are about 4 meters (12 feet) long. One end of each worm is attached to the ocean floor. The other end gathers material from the seawater.

Rather live where it's not so hot? Try the tundra. It's a cold, dry region where no trees grow. The ground just below the surface is frozen all the time!

Very few animals make their homes on the tundra. Caribou spend half of the year here. They have broad feet that help them walk in snow and dig through snow to find food. Caribou travel in large herds and are always on the move. That way they don't run out of food.

Discussion Starter

1. Could tube worms live near the ocean surface? Why or why not?

2. A pipeline was built across the tundra to move oil. Would that have hurt the caribou? What could be done to protect the tundra and the animals?

interNET CONNECTION To learn more about different environments, visit www.mhschool.com/science and enter the keyword **SETTINGS**.

Topic 2
LIFE SCIENCE

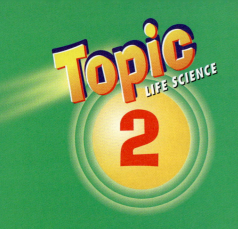

WHY IT MATTERS

You depend on other living things for food.

SCIENCE WORDS

producer an organism that makes its own food

consumer an organism that eats producers or other consumers

food chain a series of organisms that depend on one another for food

decomposer an organism that breaks down dead plant and animal material

food web several food chains that are connected

energy pyramid a diagram that shows how energy is used in an ecosystem

Food

Can three different animals eat one plant? Yes! Thomson's gazelle, the zebra, and the wildebeest all eat the same grass for food. Each animal eats a different part of the grass.

Thomson's gazelle likes the bottom part of the grass. The zebra eats the top part of the grass and the wildebeest eats the middle. Which animal do you think eats the grass first?

EXPLORE

HYPOTHESIZE People eat many different kinds of foods. Does more of the food you eat come from plants or animals? Write a hypothesis in your *Science Journal.* How might you investigate your ideas?

EXPLORE ACTIVITY

Investigate Where Food Comes From

Analyze a pizza to infer where food comes from.

MATERIALS
- Science Journal

PROCEDURES

1. **OBSERVE** Look carefully at the picture of the pizza. What types of foods do you see? Make a list in your *Science Journal*.

2. **CLASSIFY** Divide your list of foods into groups. Which foods come from plants? Which foods come from animals?

3. Plants can make their own food. Animals cannot. Look at your list of foods that come from animals. What animal does each of the foods come from? What food does that animal eat?

CONCLUDE AND APPLY

1. **CAUSE AND EFFECT** If there were no plants, which foods would be left to make pizza? (Hint: Think about what animals eat in order to survive.)

2. **INFER** Do all foods come from plants? Write down another type of food that you like to eat. See if you can trace the ingredients back to plants.

GOING FURTHER: Apply

3. **COMMUNICATE** Create a chart that shows where the ingredients in question 2 come from.

Where Does Food Come From?

The Explore Activity demonstrates that all food comes from plants. Plants are **producers** (prə dü′sərz). Producers are organisms that make their own food. For example, the plants on page 332 are producers. The three grazing animals are **consumers** (kən sü′mər). Consumers are organisms that eat producers or other consumers.

What is food? Food is material that organisms use to get energy. To make food, producers need water, sunlight, air, and minerals. Organisms that are producers include plants and algae. The cells of producers contain a special chemical. Organisms with this chemical can make food.

Producers and consumers make up a **food chain** (füd chān). A food chain is a series of organisms that depend on one another for food. Food chains start with producers. Consumers eat those producers. Other consumers eat the first consumers.

This plant is a producer. The caterpillars are consumers.

DESERT FOOD CHAIN

OCEAN FOOD CHAIN

Hawk eats snake

Snake eats mouse

Mouse eats insect

Insect eats plant

Plant makes food

Killer whale eats large fish

Large fish eats small fish

Small fish eats shellfish

Shellfish eats one-celled consumers

One-celled consumers eat one-celled producers

One-celled producers make food

READING DIAGRAMS

1. **WRITE** List the organisms that make up each food chain.
2. **DISCUSS** How are these two food chains different? How are they alike?

How Are Materials Recycled?

As living things go through their life cycles, new organisms are produced. Old organisms die. What happens to all the dead plant and animal material in an ecosystem? It must be cleaned up. **Decomposers** (dē′kəm pō′zərz) are the organisms that do the cleaning. A decomposer breaks down dead plant and animal material. It recycles chemicals so they can be used again.

Decomposers include *bacteria*. Bacteria are one-celled organisms. Some bacteria cause infections and disease. However, without bacteria, Earth would be covered by dead plant and animal material. Decomposers also include *fungi* (fun′jī). Fungi are organisms that take in chemicals from dead material. You might see fungi growing on a dead log.

When you see decomposing material, you are seeing an energy transformation. Some of the energy in the material goes to the decomposer. Some of the energy changes to heat.

Producers, consumers, and decomposers work together to recycle materials through an ecosystem. Producers use the recycled material to make new food. Consumers eat that food. When producers and consumers die, decomposers recycle the dead material. Then the cycle is repeated.

Decomposers

HYPOTHESIZE What will happen to bread and apples if they are left out for one week? Write a hypothesis in your *Science Journal*.

SAFETY: Don't open the sealed bags.

PROCEDURES

1. Put the bread in one plastic bag. Put the apple pieces in the other bag. Seal the bags.

2. **OBSERVE** Leave the materials in the bags for one week. What happens to each material?

CONCLUDE AND APPLY

1. **IDENTIFY** What evidence of decomposers do you see? Is there more than one decomposer? How do you know?

2. **INFER** Do different types of decomposers break down different types of material? Explain.

MATERIALS
- 2 self-sealing plastic bags
- apple pieces
- slice of bread
- *Science Journal*

What Is a Food Web?

Ecosystems contain more than one food chain. They contain **food webs** (füd webz). Food webs are made up of several food chains that are connected. Take a look at the desert ecosystem food web. Can you recognize the original desert food chain from page 335?

There are many food chains in this food web. The original desert food chain is just one of the chains. Which animals does it link together?

Notice how other food chains connect to the original chain. For example, try to find the cactus-jackrabbit-hawk chain.

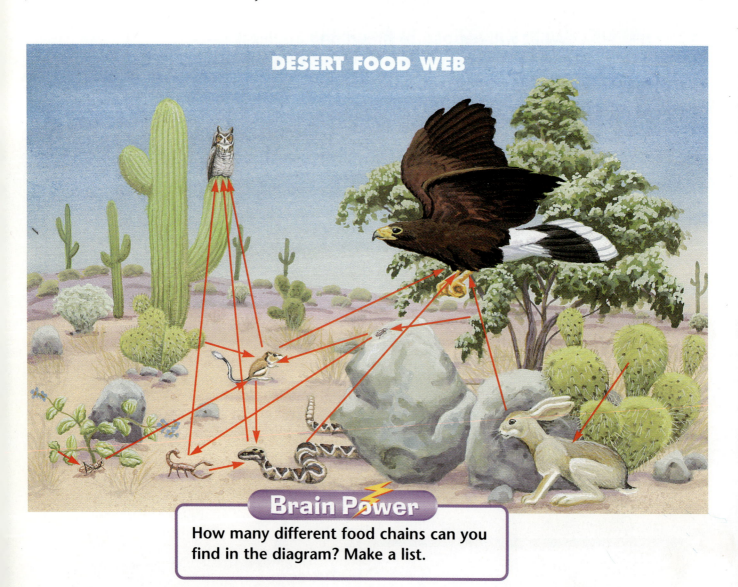

DESERT FOOD WEB

Brain Power
How many different food chains can you find in the diagram? Make a list.

An ecosystem has different kinds of organisms. Each type of organism forms its own level on an **energy pyramid** (en′ər jē pir′ə mid′). An energy pyramid is a diagram that shows how energy is used in an ecosystem.

Each level in an energy pyramid has more members in it than the level above it. There are more producers than plant-eaters. There are more plant-eaters than meat-eaters. This means that for every frog in a pond, there might be hundreds of bugs and thousands of plants.

ENERGY PYRAMID

Meat eaters

Plant eaters

Producers

WHY IT MATTERS

You are a consumer. You are part of a food web. You probably depend on many different producers and other consumers for food. You also depend on decomposers to recycle plant and animal materials in your ecosystem.

REVIEW

1. Where does food come from?
2. What is a producer? A consumer? A decomposer?
3. How is a food web different from a food chain?
4. **INFER** What does an energy pyramid tell you about a community?
5. **CRITICAL THINKING** *Evaluate* What would happen if an ecosystem had more consumers than producers? Could this ecosystem last?

WHY IT MATTERS THINK ABOUT IT
Like other organisms, you belong to a food web. Describe the food web that you are part of.

WHY IT MATTERS WRITE ABOUT IT
Draw a diagram of your food web. How do you fit into your food web?

READING SKILL All foods come from producers. Use pictures and arrows to show the events that must take place for you to have a glass of milk.

SCIENCE MAGAZINE

FOODS Around the World

Why do people in different countries eat different foods? Different foods grow in different places. Even though foods are shipped all around the world, people often eat the foods that grow near them naturally.

Europe and the Near East

Your body uses foods that contain starch and fat for energy. For thousands of years, people in Europe and the Near East have used wheat as their main starch. People near the Mediterranean grow olives that provide fat through oil. Farther north, there are not as many plants with oil. People there have traditionally used animal fat in their diet.

The Americas

Potatoes are an important starch in the Americas. Corn, or maize, was once the main starch in North America. Today most corn is fed to animals or made into sugars, oils, or chemicals. However, corn is still the main starch in Mexico.

Social Studies Link

Asia

Rice is the main starch of Southeast Asia. In northern Asia, it's too cold to grow rice. People in northern China use wheat. The Chinese may have invented pasta using wheat. The Chinese also use oil from soybeans or peanuts. In India, people use rice and wheat. Food is cooked in butter from milk or oil from sesame seeds.

The Tropics

Grasses such as wheat, rice, and corn are difficult to grow in the tropics. So are potatoes. In South and Central America, people grow a different starchy underground tuber called a yuca, manioc, or cassava. In West Africa, people get oil from palm trees. Palm oil and coconut oil are also popular in the American tropics.

DISCUSSION STARTER

1. If fats from plants are better for us than fats from animals, why have people in colder regions traditionally used animal fat?

2. Most basic foods—wheat, rice, potatoes, yuca—have very little flavor. Is this an advantage or a disadvantage? Explain.

To learn more about basic, or staple, foods, visit *www.mhschool.com/science* and enter the keyword BASIC.

interNET CONNECTION

Topic 3 LIFE SCIENCE

Roles for Living Things

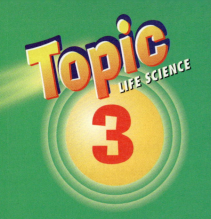

What do these fish need to survive? What do you think the plants need?

You probably know that taking care of a pet takes a lot of work. Even a plant needs some care. What would you do to take care of the living things in this aquarium?

WHY IT MATTERS

All living things depend on other living things to meet their needs for survival.

EXPLORE

HYPOTHESIZE Pets and houseplants have people to take care of them. How do plants and animals in nature get what they need to live and grow? Write a hypothesis in your *Science Journal*. How might you test your ideas?

SCIENCE WORDS

carbon dioxide and oxygen cycle the exchange of gases between producers and consumers

parasite an organism that lives in or on another organism

host the organism a parasite lives in or on

EXPLORE ACTIVITY

Investigate How Living Things Meet Their Needs

Observe an aquarium to infer how plants and animals meet their needs.

MATERIALS
- fish food
- gravel
- small guppy or goldfish
- fish net
- 2 small elodea or other water plants
- 2 L plastic drink bottle
- bottom of another drink bottle with holes
- water
- meter tape
- *Science Journal*

PROCEDURES

1. **MAKE A MODEL** Put a 3 cm layer of gravel into the plastic drink bottle. Fill the bottle about half full of water. Anchor the plants by gently pushing their roots into the gravel. Cover the bottle with the bottom of another bottle. Put the container in a place where it receives plenty of light, but do not place it directly in the Sun.

2. After 2 days, use the fish net to gently place the fish into the bottle. Add a few flakes of fish food to the bottle through one of the holes in the top. Later in the week, add some more.

3. **OBSERVE** Observe your ecosystem every few days for 4 weeks. Feed the fish twice each week. Record your observations in your *Science Journal*.

CONCLUDE AND APPLY

1. **COMPARE** How has your ecosystem changed over the 4 weeks?

2. **IDENTIFY** What did the fish need to survive? What did the plant need to survive?

3. **INFER** You probably observed bubbles in your ecosystem. What do you think those bubbles were? Where did they come from?

GOING FURTHER: Apply

4. **INFER** Did the living things in this ecosystem meet their needs? How do you know?

How Do Living Things Meet Their Needs?

The ecosystem in the Explore Activity shows how organisms depend on one another to meet their needs. The ecosystem had two populations. Each population used some of what the other put into the water. The bubbles in the water were a clue that a gas was in the water. Where did the gas come from? The plant gave off oxygen for the fish to use. The fish gave off carbon dioxide for the plant to use.

The fish and the plant take part in the **carbon dioxide and oxygen cycle** (kär′bən dī ok′sīd and ok′sə jən sī kəl). The carbon dioxide and oxygen cycle is the process of trading oxygen and carbon dioxide. This cycle is based on needs of producers and consumers. These gases are passed from one population to another in both water and land habitats. If gases were used up instead of exchanged in this cycle, living things would die. You can follow the carbon dioxide and oxygen cycle in the steps below.

Step 1 Producers give off oxygen as they make their own food.

Step 2 Consumers take in the oxygen that producers make.

Step 3 Consumers give off carbon dioxide.

Step 4 Producers take in carbon dioxide from consumers.

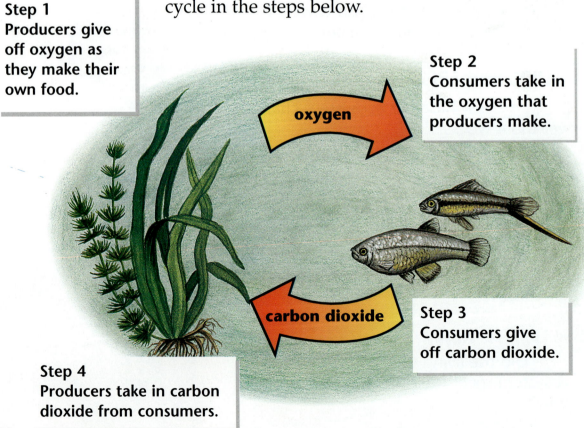

Gases are recycled in the carbon dioxide and oxygen cycle. Animals breathe in oxygen and breathe out carbon dioxide. Plants take in carbon dioxide and give off oxygen. Plants need some oxygen, too. Plants need oxygen to get energy from food. During the day, plants make oxygen and release it into the air. They also take in some oxygen. At night, plants don't make food or oxygen. They take in oxygen from the air, just like animals do.

Where does the world's oxygen supply come from? Green plants give off oxygen. Forests are big suppliers of oxygen. Trees are the world's largest oxygen-producing organisms. However, the most important source of oxygen is in the oceans. Algae make more oxygen than all the land plants in the world.

How are you a part of the carbon dioxide and oxygen cycle? You are a consumer. You breathe oxygen in and carbon dioxide out.

NATIONAL GEOGRAPHIC
FUNtastic Facts

Pitcher plants eat insects. However, sometimes ants live inside pitcher plants. The ants "fish" for insect victims in the pitcher plant. The ants also protect the plant from other insects. What other plants "work" with animals in this way?

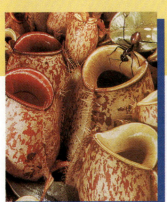

How Else Do Populations Depend on Each Other?

You know that plants and animals depend on each other for oxygen and carbon dioxide. Organisms depend on one another in other ways, too.

Sometimes two populations help each other to survive. Each type of organism depends on the other. For example, the clownfish and the sea anemone help each other.

Sea anemones are dangerous organisms. Their poison tentacles can be deadly to many kinds of fish. However, the clownfish swims near the anemone without being harmed. Its body is coated with special slime that protects it from the anemone's stingers.

The clownfish uses the anemone for protection. When it is threatened, the clownfish swims to the anemone's tentacles for safety. The anemone uses the clownfish to get food. The anemone feeds on scraps that fall out of the clownfish's mouth.

Sometimes only one of the populations depends on the other to survive. The second population isn't helped by the first.

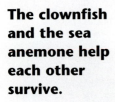

The clownfish and the sea anemone help each other survive.

Cattle egrets are birds that could find food in many places. However, they spend their time following cattle. Wherever the cattle go, the egrets follow. What does the cattle egret get from the cattle? The cattle are so big that they stir up insects and other small animals wherever they feed. The egrets follow behind the cattle to get food. The cattle aren't always helped by the egrets. They aren't harmed, either.

Sometimes one population does harm another population. A tapeworm like the one shown cannot live on its own. It lives inside the body of other organisms. Tapeworms are **parasites** (par′ə sīt′z). A parasite is an organism that lives in or on a **host** (hōst). A host is the organism that a parasite lives with.

The host of a tapeworm can be an animal or a human. The tapeworm gets food by attaching itself to the host. Then it takes in food that the host has digested. Parasites like the tapeworm harm their hosts. A tapeworm can make its host sick. In some cases it can even kill its host.

Parasites are more common than you may think. Fleas are parasites to dogs. They eat the blood of dogs as food. The dogs are harmed by the parasites, but rarely killed.

A tapeworm is a parasite.

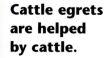

Cattle egrets are helped by cattle.

How Do Animals Help Plants Reproduce?

An oak tree makes seeds called acorns. Acorns will develop into new oak trees if they fall in the right place to grow. Most acorns fall right under the tree. Is this a good place for the acorns? No. There is not enough light to grow. Somehow the acorns must be moved to a better location.

How do the acorns move to another place? Animals help. Squirrels find the acorns. They bury the acorns in the ground to store them for winter. Most of the acorns get eaten by the squirrels, but a few of them are forgotten. They stay buried in the ground, far from the tree. They will grow into new trees.

Squirrels bury acorns to store them for winter.

Traveling Seeds

HYPOTHESIZE Animals with fur often help plants spread their seeds. How might they do this? Write a hypothesis in your *Science Journal*.

PROCEDURES

1. **PREDICT** What will happen when you toss the seeds onto the fur? Record your prediction in your *Science Journal*.

2. **EXPERIMENT** Test your prediction. Have your partner hold up the fur. Toss different seeds at it. Record the results.

MATERIALS
- seeds
- fake fur
- *Science Journal*

CONCLUDE AND APPLY

1. **IDENTIFY** Which of the seeds stuck to the fur?

2. **INFER** How might animals with fur help plants spread their seeds?

Brain Power

Some seeds can travel for miles without being helped by any animals. How do these seeds move from place to place? (Hint: Think of a dandelion seed.)

WHY IT MATTERS

You have seen how organisms depend on one another. You also depend on other organisms. You depend on plants and animals for food. You also depend on them for other things. You depend on trees for wood to make houses and furniture. You depend on plants and animals to make fabric for clothes. Do you have a pet? If you do, you depend on an animal for companionship.

REVIEW

1. How do living things meet their needs?
2. What gases are exchanged in the carbon dioxide and oxygen cycle? Who uses the gases?
3. Give an example of two organisms that depend on each other for survival.
4. **HYPOTHESIZE** What might happen to a population of oak trees if the squirrels that live nearby disappear? Why?
5. **CRITICAL THINKING Apply** What is the disadvantage of a parasite killing its host?

WHY IT MATTERS THINK ABOUT IT Describe an organism that depends on you or a person you know for its survival. How are its needs met?

WHY IT MATTERS WRITE ABOUT IT In what ways do you depend on this organism? Who else depends on this organism?

SCIENCE MAGAZINE

People Who

Everyone needs help sometime. Like plants and other animals, people depend on one another. That's why communities have special people to lend a hand.

What if a house catches on fire? What would people do without the community fire department? The home might be destroyed. A family might be hurt, too. Instead, the firefighters put out the fire . . . safely.

People provide other services for citizens—the people who live in a community. Some people are police officers. Others collect the garbage or fix holes in the streets. Still others drive buses or run recycling centers.

People have other helpful jobs in their communities. They may teach or help homeless people find somewhere to live. They may be doctors, nurses, or counselors who work at the community clinic.

Community services are expensive. To pay for them, citizens pay taxes. The money they pay buys the services they need.

Social Studies Link

Need People

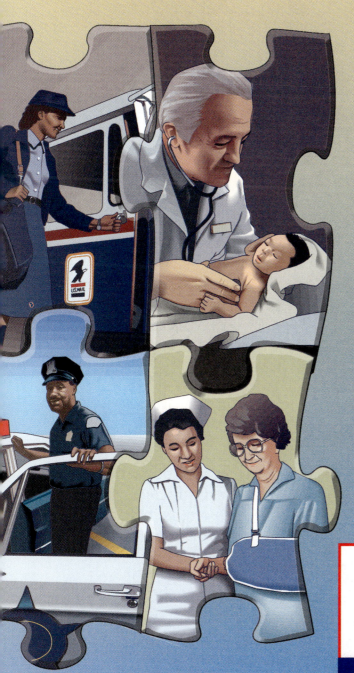

People in a community also buy individual services and goods. They buy gas, electricity, telephone, and cable services from local companies. They buy food, clothing, and other goods from local stores. The money they pay helps the community grow.

Which job would you like to do in your community? Why?

DISCUSSION STARTER

1. Why do people pay taxes?
2. What would happen if many people in the community wanted to be police officers, but no one wanted to collect the garbage?

To learn more about jobs, visit **www.mhschool.com/science** and enter the keyword WORKERS.

interNET CONNECTION

CHAPTER 11 REVIEW

SCIENCE WORDS

community p.324
consumers p.334
decomposers p.336
ecosystem p.324
food chain p.334
food web p.338
habitat p.324
host p.347
carbon dioxide and oxygen cycle p.344
parasite p.347
population p.324
producers p.334

USING SCIENCE WORDS

Number a paper from 1 to 10. Fill in 1 to 5 with words from the list above.

1. A series of organisms that rely on each other for food is called a ___?___.
2. Oxygen is traded for carbon dioxide in the ___?___.
3. A parasite lives in or on a ___?___.
4. A group of food chains that are connected together make a ___?___.
5. Dead plant and animal material is broken down by ___?___.

6–10. Pick five words from the list above that were not used in 1 to 5 and use each in a sentence.

UNDERSTANDING SCIENCE IDEAS

11. How is it possible to grow a plant from the rain forest inside of a house in the desert?
12. Producers can get along without consumers. Why can't consumers get along without producers?

USING IDEAS AND SKILLS

13. **READING SKILL: REPRESENT TEXT IN DIFFERENT WAYS** Read the second paragraph on page 348. Use pictures and arrows to represent the ideas in the text.

14. **DEFINE** Using your observations, write a definition of an aquarium ecosystem.

15. **THINKING LIKE A SCIENTIST** Most scientists think that plants appeared on Earth before animals. Suggest reasons why they think this is true.

PROBLEMS and PUZZLES

Habitat Hideouts Look around outdoors for a rock or cardboard lying on the ground. Is there a habitat underneath? Wear a pair of gloves and gently lift up the rock. Is anything growing? Do you see any life forms? Why is this their habitat? Write down your observations.

CHAPTER 12
KEEPING IN BALANCE

Earth is carefully balanced. It has many parts that must work together. A change in one part of the system affects other parts. What kinds of changes might take place? How do living things survive these changes?

In Chapter 12 you will compare and contrast different environments. When you compare two things, you tell how they are alike. When you contrast two things, you tell how they are not alike.

Topic 4
LIFE SCIENCE

WHY IT MATTERS

Living things compete against each other to meet their needs.

SCIENCE WORDS

competition when one organism works against another to get what it needs to live

predator an animal that hunts other animals for food

prey the animal a predator hunts

niche the job or role an organism has in an ecosystem

Competition

Who gets the worm? All of the young birds want it. Which one will get it? The loudest bird? The bird that looks hungriest? Birds compete to get worms. In what ways do you compete in your own life? What do you think is the best way to get something you need? If you were a baby bird, what would you do?

EXPLORE

HYPOTHESIZE You know that space is one of the needs of living things. When there are too many people in one place it gets uncomfortable! What happens when there are too many plants in one place? Does the amount of space available affect the way plants grow? Write a hypothesis in your *Science Journal*.

EXPLORE ACTIVITY

Investigate How Much Room Plants Need

Explore how crowding affects how plants grow.

MATERIALS
- soil
- bean seeds
- 4 milk cartons
- measuring cup
- water
- marker
- masking tape
- scissors
- Science Journal

PROCEDURES

1. Cut the tops from the milk cartons. Use the masking tape and the marker to label the cartons A to D. Carefully punch 3 drainage holes in the bottom of each carton. Use the measuring cup to fill each carton with the same amount of soil.

2. **USE VARIABLES** Plant 3 bean seeds in carton A. Plant 6 bean seeds in carton B. Plant 12 bean seeds in carton C and 24 bean seeds in carton D.

3. **PREDICT** What do you think each carton will look like in 14 days? Draw a picture in your *Science Journal* that shows your predictions.

4. **EXPERIMENT** Place the cartons in a well-lighted area. Water the plants every 2 days. Use the same amount of water for each carton.

CONCLUDE AND APPLY

1. **COMPARE** How many plants are there in each carton? How do the plants in carton D compare to the plants in the other cartons?

2. **IDENTIFY** For what things are the plants in each container competing?

3. **EXPLAIN** How did the number of plants in carton D affect the ability of each plant to get what it needs?

GOING FURTHER: Problem Solving

4. **EXPERIMENT** How could you test how much space pet gerbils need? Write a plan.

How Much Room Do Plants Need?

The owl is a predator. The lizard is its prey.

The Explore Activity shows that **competition** (kom′pi tish′ən) for space affects how plants grow. Competition occurs when one organism works against another to get what it needs to live. Organisms may compete for space, water, food, or some other need.

Desert plants compete for water. A cactus soaks up all of the moisture in a single area. No other plants can grow in this area. Rabbits compete for food. If there are too many rabbits, all of the grass will be eaten. Some of the rabbits won't survive.

Predators (pred′ə tərz) also compete. Predators are animals that hunt for food. Predators compete for **prey** (prā). Prey are the animals that predators hunt. Prey try to escape from predators. Predators compete with each other. Hawks, owls, and snakes all compete to catch lizards for food.

For example, there are many types of pigeons in the forests of New Guinea. Each type of pigeon has a different niche in the forest ecosystem. They avoid competition by living in different places and eating different foods.

The Victoria crowned pigeon is one type of pigeon found in New Guinea. The niche of Victoria crowned pigeons includes eating fruits, berries, and large seeds. They nest in trees, and search for food on the ground of the forest.

WHY IT MATTERS

As a living thing, you have a niche in your ecosystem. Your niche includes the roles you have at home and at school. How is your niche different from the niches of other animals and people in the ecosystem?

Victoria crowned pigeon

REVIEW

1. What is competition?
2. What things do organisms compete for?
3. What is a niche?
4. **INFER** Why do some ecosystems have more types of organisms than others?
5. **CRITICAL THINKING Apply** Does a desert have more types of organisms than a rain forest? How do you know?

WHY IT MATTERS THINK ABOUT IT
Describe the niche you fill in your ecosystem.

WHY IT MATTERS WRITE ABOUT IT
How might your niche change as you grow?

SCIENCE MAGAZINE

ENOUGH to Go Around

Life's a contest! Who will win? A bluebird and sparrow both compete for space to build their nests. A fast-growing maple tree and slower-growing dogwood compete for the sunlight they both need. Oil competes with coal and nuclear power as an energy source for electric power plants.

There's a problem. There's a limited amount of space for birds, sunlight for trees, and energy for people! If we don't cut back on our uses of some of our resources, someday they'll be gone!

How can we use energy today and know we'll have enough to go around in the future? We can choose alternate, or replacement, energy resources. It takes Earth millions of years to create coal, oil, and gas. They are nonrenewable resources.

Science, Technology, and Society

Solar energy is renewable. It comes from the Sun! The Sun's heat can boil water and provide steam energy. Solar power is already used to run small calculators and watches. It can be used to run many more things.

Wind energy is another renewable resource. The wind can be used to turn windmills. They in turn run big machines that produce electricity!

Water is a renewable resource. The power of fast-running rivers can be used to run machines and create electricity.

What other ways can we conserve our resources? How can we make sure there's always enough to go around?

DISCUSSION STARTER

1. Name as many ways as you can that people, plants, and animals use energy from the Sun.
2. For what other kinds of things do people, plants, and animals compete?

To learn more about competition, visit **www.mhschool.com/science** and enter the keyword COMPETE.

interNET CONNECTION

Topic 5
LIFE SCIENCE

WHY IT MATTERS

Certain characteristics allow living things to survive in their environment.

SCIENCE WORDS

adaptation a characteristic that helps an organism survive in its environment

camouflage an adaptation that allows animals to blend into their surroundings

Fit for Surviving

Could a goose perch on a tree branch? Why or why not? What kind of feet would be best for perching on a tree branch? Parts of animals are like tools. Each part has a job to do. The job of goose feet is to paddle through water. Compare the feet of a goose to the feet of an eagle. How are they different? What jobs do you think the eagle's feet have?

EXPLORE

HYPOTHESIZE You know that animals are made up of different parts. All birds have beaks, but different kinds of birds have different kinds of beaks. How does a bird's beak help it eat the foods it needs? Write a hypothesis in your *Science Journal*. How might you test your ideas?

Design Your Own Experiment

HOW DOES THE SHAPE OF A BIRD'S BEAK AFFECT WHAT IT EATS?

MATERIALS
- chopsticks
- spoon
- tweezers
- clothespin
- drinking straw
- rubber worm
- peanut in shell
- rice
- water in paper cup
- *Science Journal*

PROCEDURES

1. **PLAN** How can you model how a bird's beak helps it to eat? Look at the materials given to you. How will you use them? Record your plan in your *Science Journal*.

2. **COLLECT DATA** Follow your plan. Be sure to record all your observations in your *Science Journal*. You might want to create a chart in which to record your data.

CONCLUDE AND APPLY

1. **COMPARE** Share your chart with other groups. How are your results similar? How are they different?

2. **DRAW CONCLUSIONS** Are some tools better suited to different jobs? How do you know?

GOING FURTHER: Apply

3. **INFER** How might the shape of a bird's beak help it to eat the foods it needs?

How Does the Shape of a Bird's Beak Affect What It Eats?

The Explore Activity shows that tools work in different ways. Some tools are good for picking up small things. Other tools are better for picking up large things. Parts of organisms also work like tools. A bird uses its beak as a tool for eating. Different beak shapes are suited to different kinds of food.

The honeycreeper is a kind of bird. There are different types of honeycreepers. Each type has a beak that is shaped differently. Each beak shape is an **adaptation** (ad′əp tā′shən). An adaptation is a special characteristic that helps an organism survive. How do different kinds of beaks help honeycreepers survive?

THE HONEYCREEPER BIRD

Each type of honeycreeper has one of these three basic beak shapes.

A long, curved beak is good for eating nectar from flowers.

A beak that is short, thick, and strong is just right for eating seeds and nuts.

A straight beak is good for eating insects.

Hawaiian honeycreepers live only on the islands of Hawaii.

READING CHARTS

1. **DISCUSS** How are honeycreepers alike? How are they different?
2. **WRITE** Compare the beak of a honeycreeper that eats seeds to the beak of a honeycreeper that eats insects.

Honeycreeper beaks are just one type of adaptation. There are many other types. In fact, most organisms have a variety of adaptations. Each adaptation helps the organism survive.

How is the wool of a lamb an adaptation? It keeps the lamb warm. A warm coat helps the lamb survive cold winter days. A giraffe's long neck is an adaptation, too. It helps the giraffe find food in high places. Finding food that others can't reach increases the giraffe's chances of survival. A frog has a long, sticky tongue. It helps the frog catch insects. Catching insects helps the frog get the food energy it needs to survive. The bright coloring of a flower is an adaptation. It attracts insects that help the flower reproduce. Reproduction makes sure that this type of plant survives.

A frog's long, sticky tongue is an adaptation.

This Indian leaf butterfly uses camouflage to protect itself. With its wings folded up, it looks like a dead leaf. Can you find the butterfly?

What Adaptations Help Protect Living Things?

Adaptations help organisms survive in different ways. Some of the most important adaptations are for protection. Organisms need protection from the weather and from their predators.

The shell of a turtle is an example of an adaptation that protects a living thing. When a turtle needs protection, it curls up inside of its shell. A rabbit may use its speed for protection. If a predator comes too close, the rabbit can run to safety. Rabbits also use **camouflage** (kam′ə fläzh) for protection. Camouflage is an adaptation that allows an organism to blend in with its environment. White rabbits blend in with the snow. Brown rabbits match their forest habitat.

Brain Power
What purpose do you think the eyespots of this butterfly have?

SKILL BUILDER

Skill: Observing

IDENTIFYING PROPERTIES OF AN ENVIRONMENT

You know that camouflage is one way animals keep safe. In this activity you will observe an area of your classroom. When you observe something, you use one or more of your senses to learn about the properties of objects. You will use your observations of your classroom to help you design an animal that could hide in that environment.

MATERIALS
- construction paper
- crayons
- cotton balls
- yarn
- scissors
- tape
- *Science Journal*

PROCEDURES

1. **OBSERVE** Your teacher will help you select an area to observe. This area is the environment for the organism that you will design. What do you notice about the area? Record your observations in your *Science Journal*.

2. **PLAN** Discuss your observations with your group members. Make a list of features that would help an organism hide in this environment.

3. Use the materials given to you to create a plant or animal that will blend into its surroundings. Put your plant or animal into its environment.

CONCLUDE AND APPLY

1. **OBSERVE** Look for the organisms that your classmates designed. What are the features of each environment? Can you find the camouflaged organism? What characteristics help it to blend in?

2. **COMMUNICATE** Describe the characteristics of the organism that you made. Explain why you included each one.

3. **INFER** Some animals can change the color of their body covering. When might they do this? Why?

How Do Organisms in Different Environments Adapt?

Organisms in different environments have different types of adaptations. For example, a wolf that lives in a cold forest has a thick coat. A wolf that lives in a hot desert has a much thinner coat.

ADAPTATIONS IN DIFFERENT ENVIRONMENTS

	Desert	Arctic Tundra	River
Trees	A mesquite tree has deep roots.	No trees grow in the cold tundra.	A cottonwood tree has shallow roots.
Bears	No bears live in the desert.	A polar bear has thick white fur.	A black bear has black fur.
Birds	A roadrunner has brown feathers.	A snowy owl has white feathers.	A duck has waterproof feathers.

READING CHARTS

1. **DISCUSS** Why does the cottonwood tree have shallow roots? Why does the mesquite tree have deep roots?
2. **WRITE** Which environment has the greatest number of different organisms? Why do you think this is so?

WHY IT MATTERS

People also have special adaptations that suit their environment. Your hands are a special adaptation. You can use your hands to do things that no other organism can do. For example, you can paint a picture, throw a ball, or play the piano. What other things can you do with your hands?

REVIEW

1. What is an adaptation?
2. What is camouflage? Give an example of camouflage.
3. Describe some adaptations that protect organisms.
4. **OBSERVE** Look at the picture of the frog on page 365. Write a description of the frog. What adaptations help it survive?
5. **CRITICAL THINKING** *Analyze* Compare reptiles that live in the desert and the rainforest. In what ways would you expect them to be different? How might they be the same?

WHY IT MATTERS THINK ABOUT IT Describe your favorite animal. What environment does it live in?

WHY IT MATTERS WRITE ABOUT IT What are some of your favorite animal's adaptations?

READING SKILL Compare and contrast the adaptations of your favorite animal with the adaptations of a giraffe. How are they alike? How are they different?

SCIENCE MAGAZINE

LEAPIN' LIZARDS!

Lizards are the favorite food of snakes, hawks, and other animals. Even so, lizards are pretty good at staying alive.

Some Lizards Disappear

The leaf-tailed gecko looks like a bump on a tree. It uses camouflage to blend in with the tree bark and moss found in its forest habitat. The gecko sits quietly all day, hiding in plain sight. At night it searches for food.

Some Lizards Scare Predators

When the frilled lizard of Australia is attacked, it raises the stiff skin around its neck. It hisses and lashes its tail. Even large snakes back off… wouldn't you?

What does the Texas horned lizard do when grabbed by an attacker? This lizard squirts blood out of its eyes! Most attackers let go . . . very quickly!

A Closer Look

Some Lizards Hide Out

The chuckwalla lives in Mexico and the southwestern United States. When it sees a predator, this lizard slips into a crack between two rocks. Then it puffs itself full of air. Even if the predator does find the chuckwalla, it can't pull the lizard out!

Some Lizards Run

Most lizards run fast, but the basilisk of Central and South America even runs on water! How? It has special scales on the bottoms of its rear feet. If the basilisk slows down, it sinks into the water and must swim to safety!

DISCUSSION STARTER

1. Why did lizards develop these ways to escape from their predators?

2. What would happen if hawks learned how to spot geckos sitting on branches?

To learn more about lizards, visit www.mhschool.com/science and enter the keyword LIZARDS.

Topic 6
LIFE SCIENCE

WHY IT MATTERS

A change in an ecosystem affects the organisms that live there.

SCIENCE WORDS

perish to not survive

relocate to find a new home

endangered in danger of becoming extinct

extinct when there are no more of a certain plant or animal

Things Change

Before the spring of 1980, Mt. St. Helens was a sleeping volcano. Bears and elk roamed its deep green forests. Fish swam in its cool, clear streams. Wildflowers bloomed on its slopes.

Then, on May 18, 1980, Mt. St. Helens erupted. A huge eruption changed local habitats forever. How do you think these changes affected wildlife in the area?

EXPLORE

HYPOTHESIZE A big storm or volcanic eruption can cause a lot of change in a short amount of time. How do changes like these affect the living things in a particular area? Write a hypothesis in your *Science Journal*. How might you use a model to investigate your ideas?

EXPLORE ACTIVITY

Investigate What Happens When Ecosystems Change

Model what may happen when an ecosystem changes.

MATERIALS
- 3 Predator cards:
  Red hawk
  Blue owl
  Green snake
- 12 Prey cards:
  4 red
  4 blue
  4 green
- *Science Journal*

PROCEDURES

1. Make the 3 predator and 12 prey cards listed in the Materials. Give 1 predator card to each player. Stack the prey cards in the deck.

2. The object of the game is to get all 4 prey cards. To play:
   - Predators take turns drawing a prey card from the deck. Keep prey cards that match the color of your predator card. Return all other prey cards to the pile. Play until one predator gets all 4 matching prey cards.

3. **EXPERIMENT** Add a card that says "fire" to the deck of prey cards. Play the game again. Any predator who draws the fire card must go out of the game. Return the fire card to the deck. The other two players continue to play until a predator gets all 4 prey cards or all players are out.

CONCLUDE AND APPLY

1. **COMPARE AND CONTRAST** What happened when you played the game the first time? What happened the second time?

2. **CAUSE AND EFFECT** The fire card represented a change to the ecosystem. What effect did the change have?

3. **INFER** What may happen when an ecosystem changes?

GOING FURTHER: Problem Solving

4. **PREDICT** What might happen if you changed the number of prey cards?

What Happens When Ecosystems Change?

The Explore Activity demonstrates that ecosystems can change. When change occurs, the organisms that live in that ecosystem are affected. Some have trouble surviving.

How did habitats near Spirit Lake change? After the eruption the forest was buried in ash. When it rained the ash turned muddy. Then the ash hardened into a tough crust. Plants were killed under the thick ash crust. Other living things that lived near the ground had their habitats destroyed. A wind of hot steam and rock blasted the area. The wind lifted trees right out of the ground. Organisms that lived on or near trees had their habitats destroyed.

Animals that roam the forest also lost their habitats. Some moved on to find new habitats far from Mt. St. Helens. Others could not find new habitats. Most of these organisms lost their lives.

These photographs show Spirit Lake on Mt. Saint Helens before and after the volcanic eruption.

Over time, some organisms found new habitats. The fireweed plant began to grow right through the cracks in the crust. As one organism moved back in, others followed. Seeds from different plants traveled through the air. They found places to grow under uprooted tree stumps. Squirrels that were hiding underground came out. Other organisms hiding underground also appeared. After a few years, a new ecosystem began to form on the crust of ash. It is different from the ecosystem that was there before.

A volcanic eruption is one event that can change an ecosystem. A flood or drought can change an ecosystem, too. Floods are caused by heavy rains or snow. Rivers rise up over their banks, and the rising water covers dry land. A drought is the opposite of a flood. During a drought it doesn't rain for weeks or months. Rivers and lakes dry up. Wet places become dry. Other natural disasters, such as fires, earthquakes, and storms, can also change an ecosystem.

As the years pass, the green forests may return to Mt. St. Helens. The wildflowers and animals may return, too. How long might it take?

How Do Ecosystems Come Back?

After a big change, ecosystems usually come back. A fire can destroy almost all the habitats in a forest. How does a forest come back after all its habitats are destroyed? There are several stages the forest must go through.

Stage 1 Habitat destruction
Bulbs and seeds may survive the fire. They begin to grow in the ash.

Stage 2 Grasses
Over time, grasses cover the bare ground. The grasses add nutrients to the soil. They also provide a home for insects. The insects attract larger animals.

Stage 3 Larger plants
Small trees begin to grow. The trees block the Sun. Without light the grasses begin to die.

Stage 4 Forest
Small trees are replaced by different, larger trees. The forest is the final stage.

READING DIAGRAMS

1. **DISCUSS** What happens to a forest right after it is destroyed?
2. **DISCUSS** Why do animals return after the grasses and insects instead of before them?

How Do Organisms Respond to Change?

Organisms may respond to change in one of three ways. Some organisms respond to a change in their habitat by adapting. Adapting means adjusting to the new habitat. The fireweed on Mt. St. Helens was covered by crust. It adapted to its new habitat by growing through the crust.

Some organisms **perish** (per′ish). Organisms that perish do not survive. A turtle may survive a fire. Where will it find food after the fire? If it cannot meet its needs, it may not survive. Some organisms **relocate** (rē lō′kāt). An organism that relocates finds a new home. Trees were destroyed on Mt. Saint Helens. Birds that lived in the trees could fly to new trees.

This box turtle survived a forest fire.

Dodo birds once covered the island of Mauritius near Africa. They became extinct in 1680.

Habitat destruction and overcrowding are not the only threats to organisms. Other threats include hunting and pollution. In some cases, organisms become **endangered** (en dān′jərd). An endangered organism is one that has very few of its kind still alive. Endangered organisms may become **extinct** (ek stingkt′). Extinct means that there are no more of that type of organism alive. Extinct animals include the dodo bird and the saber-toothed tiger.

Crowd Control

HYPOTHESIZE What happens when the same number of organisms move into a smaller habitat? Write a hypothesis in your *Science Journal*.

MATERIALS
- 20 paper clips
- small box
- small book
- *Science Journal*

PROCEDURES

1. Toss the paper clips into the box. Remove any two paper clips that touch each other.

2. Gather the paper clips that remain from step 1 and toss them a second time. Again, remove all paper clips that touch. Repeat the process until all the paper clips are gone. Record the number of tosses you made in your *Science Journal*.

3. **EXPERIMENT** Play the game again. This time put a book into the box to make the box smaller.

CONCLUDE AND APPLY

INFER What happens when you crowd organisms together? How do their chances of survival change?

WHY IT MATTERS

How do endangered organisms affect your life? When an organism becomes extinct, it is gone forever. Everyone would notice if a large animal like the Bengal tiger were to disappear. Small organisms are important, too. Many medicines are made from plants. If plants become extinct, they can't be used to make medicines.

The Bengal tiger lives in India. Hunters have killed almost all of this kind of tiger. Today Bengal tigers live in protected national parks.

REVIEW

1. What causes ecosystems to change? What happens when an ecosystem changes?

2. How does a forest recover from destruction?

3. How do organisms respond to habitat changes?

4. **COMMUNICATE** What is the difference between endangered organisms and extinct organisms?

5. **CRITICAL THINKING** *Evaluate* A forest is cut down to build a parking lot. Why is this habitat destruction more serious than if there had been a forest fire?

WHY IT MATTERS THINK ABOUT IT
Describe an endangered organism that you would want to save.

WHY IT MATTERS WRITE ABOUT IT
Write an article for the newspaper. Tell why it is important to save this endangered organism.

SCIENCE MAGAZINE

A Closer Look

TOO MANY RABBITS!

Rabbits are cute and cuddly. There could never be too many, right? Wrong! Ask people in Australia. In the late 1800s, people first took rabbits there, and let them go free.

Before too long, the country had 600 million rabbits! They ate grass until the fields were bare, causing erosion. Sheep and other grass-eating animals starved.

In the 1950s, scientists used a virus to kill nearly all the rabbits. The few that lived had more babies, so ferrets were brought in to kill the rabbits.

The ferrets spread a disease to cattle and deer. Scientists used a different virus to kill the ferrets.

Since 1995, a new virus has killed most of the rabbits. Some people worry that a few rabbits will survive, reproduce, and take over Australia again.

DISCUSSION STARTER

1. Why do you think the rabbits became such a big problem in Australia?
2. What should scientists know before they bring in one kind of organism to get rid of another kind of organism?

To learn more about rabbits, visit *www.mhschool.com/science* and enter the keyword BUNNY.

interNET CONNECTION

CHAPTER 12 REVIEW

SCIENCE WORDS

adaptation p.364
camouflage p.366
competition p.356
endangered p.378
extinct p.378
niche p.358
predator p.356
prey p.356

USING SCIENCE WORDS

Number a paper from 1 to 10. Fill in 1 to 5 with words from the list above.

1. The white fur of the polar bear is an example of __?__.
2. A special characteristic that helps an organism survive is a(n) __?__.
3. An organism that could become extinct is __?__.
4. An animal that hunts is a __?__.
5. Organisms that all want the same thing are in __?__.

6–10. Pick five words from the list above. Include all words that were not used in 1 to 5. Use each word in a sentence.

UNDERSTANDING SCIENCE IDEAS

11. One group of rabbits lives on an island without predators. A second group on a different island lives with predators. Which group is more likely to be faster runners? Explain.
12. The walking stick insect looks just like a twig. What does this adaptation tell you about the insect's habitat?

USING IDEAS AND SKILLS

13. **READING SKILL: COMPARE AND CONTRAST** Look at page 374. Compare and contrast the two pictures of Spirit Lake on this page.
14. **OBSERVE** Draw a picture of your favorite animal. How many adaptations can you count on the animal? What purpose does each adaptation serve?
15. **THINKING LIKE A SCIENTIST** How can people build roads to cause as little habitat destruction as possible? Think of some ways to do this.

PROBLEMS and PUZZLES

Color Blind How does color help protect animals? Find a grassy area. Bring 24 plain toothpicks, 24 green toothpicks, and 24 red toothpicks. Have a friend throw the toothpicks on the grass. How many toothpicks can you pick up in one minute? Which colors did you pick the most of? Which color was hardest to see?

UNIT 6 REVIEW

USING SCIENCE WORDS

adaptation p.364
camouflage p.366
decomposer p.336
endangered p.378
extinct p.378
food web p.338
habitat p.324
host p.347
niche p.358
parasite p.347
population p.324
predator p.356
prey p.356
producers p.334

Number a paper from 1 to 10. Beside each number write the word or words that best completes the sentence.

1. The place where a plant or an animal lives is its __?__.

2. Organisms that make their own food are __?__.

3. Dead plant and animal material may be broken down by __?__.

4. A flea on a dog is an example of a __?__.

5. A parasite lives in or on a __?__.

6. An animal that hunts other animals is called a __?__.

7. The shell of a turtle is an example of an __?__ that protects a living thing.

8. A rabbit's white fur provides __?__ in the snow.

9. If there are only a few of one kind of plant, then that plant is __?__.

10. If there were no more blue whales, they would be __?__.

UNDERSTANDING SCIENCE IDEAS

Write 11 to 15. For each number write the letter for the best answer. You may wish to use the hints provided.

11. What is probably NOT found in a pond ecosystem?
    a. cactus
    b. frog
    c. heron
    d. algae
    (Hint: Read pages 326-327.)

12. Which of the following is a consumer?
    a. an ant
    b. a mushroom
    c. a lettuce plant
    d. an apple tree
    (Hint: Read page 334.)

13. Producers and consumers exchange carbon dioxide and
    a. food
    b. water
    c. habitats
    d. oxygen
    (Hint: Read page 344.)

14. Which of the following might survive best in the Arctic tundra?
    a. a cottonwood tree
    b. a mesquite tree
    c. a polar bear
    d. a road runner
    (Hint: Read page 368.)

15. Which of the following animals is now extinct?
    a. dodo bird
    b. pigeon
    c. blue whale
    d. elephant
    (Hint: Read page 379.)

UNIT 6 REVIEW

USING IDEAS AND SKILLS

16. What are three plants and three animals that share your habitat?

17. **DEFINE** Make a list of different adaptations you have learned about in this unit. Using your list, write your own definition of adaptation.

18. Give an example of how animals help plants to reproduce.

THINKING LIKE A SCIENTIST

19. **OBSERVE** Jungle birds often have bright colors. What colors do city birds usually have? Explain why.

20. How can fire change an ecosystem?

WRITING IN YOUR JOURNAL

SCIENCE IN YOUR LIFE
Make a list of some insect members of your ecosystem's community. How are these insects important to your ecosystem?

PRODUCT ADS
Sometimes insects, such as ants, can become pests. Ads for products that kill pests often say that the products are very strong and will get rid of all pests. Is this always a good thing? How might destroying a pest affect other living things in an ecosystem?

HOW SCIENTISTS WORK
Scientists observe living things to learn how they affect each other. Scientists also study how living things are affected by the nonliving parts of their ecosystems. Why do you think it is important for scientists to learn about these things?

Design your own Experiment

What animals (not pets) in your neighborhood use camouflage? Plan to make a survey of animals in your neighborhood to find out. Tell what characteristics allow each animal to blend in with its surroundings.

interNET CONNECTION

For help in reviewing this unit, visit www.mhschool.com/science

UNIT 6 REVIEW

PROBLEMS and PUZZLES

Competing Birds

Study competition between different kinds of birds. With the help of a parent or teacher, build a bird feeder from a plastic milk jug or aluminum pie pan. Place bird seed, sunflower seeds, and cracker crumbs in the feeder. Observe the different birds that visit the feeder. What kind of food does each bird eat? Do all the birds compete for the same food? Do some birds avoid competition by eating different foods? Write a report that tells what you learn from your observations.

Seeds and Soil

HYPOTHESIZE

Do bean seeds grow better in sandy soil or potting soil? Write a hypothesis.

EXPERIMENT

Plan an experiment that will test your hypothesis. What materials will you need? What variables do you need to control? What variable do you need to change? Once you have a plan approved by your teacher, try your experiment.

ANALYZE THE RESULTS

Write a report that summarizes your observations. What conclusions can you draw? List three questions you would like to answer next.

Active Algae

Place some green pond water in a clear jar. Add some tap water that has sat out overnight. Cover the jar with foil. Cut a small hole in the foil and place the jar in a window. Make sure the hole in the foil faces the sunlight. After a few hours, carefully lift the cover off the jar. What happened? Why?

REFERENCE SECTION

TP2 DIAGRAM BUILDERS

Building a Food Web
Illustrated plastic overlays that show how living things depend on each other for food

R1 HANDBOOK

Lessons in safety and skills in making measurements and observations to use anytime with this book

R27 GLOSSARY

Meanings of the Science Words used in this book

R39 INDEX

An alphabetical listing with page numbers for the topics in this book

DIAGRAM BUILDERS

Building a Food Web

All living things need food. Plants get energy from the Sun's light. They use it to make food. Most other living things get energy by taking in food. One living thing becomes the food for another. **In the diagram on the next page, which living things are food for others?**

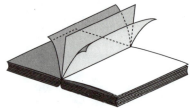

BASE

To answer the question, lift up all the plastic overlays (1, 2, 3). The page beneath them is the base. The base shows a food chain. It is made up of many organisms that depend on each other for food.
What happens to each living thing in this chain?

OVERLAY 1

1 Now drop overlay 1 onto the base. You see a second food chain. Describe it.
What do the two food chains have in common?

OVERLAY 2

2 Now drop overlay 2 onto overlay 1. You see a third food chain. Describe it.
What do the three food chains have in common?

OVERLAY 3

3 Now drop overlay 3 onto overlay 2. You see a food web. It shows how all the food chains are connected.
How are all the food chains connected?

SUMMARIZE

How many different food chains can you find in this web? List them.

BASE: Start with a food chain.

DIAGRAM BUILDERS
Activities

1. Make a Model

You need: spool of yarn, scissors, paper

In a group of ten or more, write the name of each organism from the food web on a sheet of paper. Write one name on a sheet. Hand out the sheets to ten group members. The students with papers should arrange themselves to show food chains. Other students help by tying a length of yarn from person to person to form the chain. (Tie a loop and knot around each person's wrist.) Decide how to connect the chains into a web.

2. Cause and Effect

Take out one of the organisms from the model above. What happens to the rest of the food web? Put the organism back and take out another. What happens this time? Repeat several times. What happens if a second hawk joins the food web?

3. Write an Explanation

What if there was no rain for a long time? The grass would dry up and much of it may die. What would happen to the food web? Write your ideas.

REFERENCE SECTION

HANDBOOK

MEASUREMENTS R2
SAFETY R4
COLLECT DATA
- HAND LENS R6
- MICROSCOPE R7
- COMPASS R8
- TELESCOPE R9
- CAMERA, TAPE RECORDER, MAP, AND COMPASS . . . R10

MAKE MEASUREMENTS
- LENGTH R11
- TIME R12
- VOLUME R13
- MASS R14
- WEIGHT/FORCE R16
- TEMPERATURE R17

MAKE OBSERVATIONS
- WEATHER R18
- SYSTEMS R19

REPRESENT DATA
- GRAPHS R20
- MAPS R22
- TABLES AND CHARTS R23

USE TECHNOLOGY
- COMPUTER R24
- CALCULATOR R26

GLOSSARY R27

INDEX R39

MEASUREMENTS

Temperature

1. The temperature is 77 degrees Fahrenheit.
2. That is the same as 25 degrees Celsius.
3. Water boils at 212 degrees Fahrenheit.
4. Water freezes at 0 degrees Celsius.

Length and Area

1. This classroom is 10 meters wide and 20 meters long.
2. That means the area is 200 square meters.

Mass and Weight

1. That baseball bat weighs 32 ounces.
2. 32 ounces is the same as 2 pounds.
3. The mass of the bat is 907 grams.

Volume of Fluids

1. This bottle of juice has a volume of 1 liter.
2. That is a little more than 1 quart.

Weight/Force

I weigh 85 pounds. That is a force of 380.8 newtons.

Rate

1. She can walk 20 meters in 5 seconds.
2. That means her speed is 4 meters per second.

Table of Measurements

SI (International System) of Units

Temperature
Water freezes at 0 degrees Celsius (°C) and boils at 100°C.

Length and Distance
10 millimeters (mm) = 1 centimeter (cm)
100 centimeters = 1 meter (m)
1,000 meters = 1 kilometer (km)

Volume
1 cubic centimeter (cm³) = 1 milliliter (mL)
1,000 milliliters = 1 liter (L)

Mass
1,000 milligrams (mg) = 1 gram (g)
1,000 grams = 1 kilogram (kg)

Area
1 square kilometer (km²) = l km x l km
1 hectare = 10,000 square meters (m²)

Rate
m/s = meters per second
km/h = kilometers per hour

Force
1 newton (N) = 1 kg x m/s²

English System of Units

Temperature
Water freezes at 32 degrees Fahrenheit (°F) and boils at 212°F.

Length and Distance
12 inches (in.) = 1 foot (ft)
3 feet = 1 yard (yd)
5,280 feet = 1 mile (mi)

Volume of Fluids
8 fluid ounces (fl oz) = 1 cup (c)
2 cups = 1 pint (pt)
2 pints = 1 quart (qt)
4 quarts = 1 gallon (gal)

Weight
16 ounces (oz) = 1 pound (lb)
2,000 pounds = 1 ton (T)

Rate
mph = miles per hour

SAFETY

In the Classroom

The most important part of doing any experiment is doing it safely. You can be safe by paying attention to your teacher and doing your work carefully. Here are some other ways to stay safe while you do experiments.

Before the Experiment

- Read all of the directions. Make sure you understand them. When you see ▨, be sure to follow the safety rule.
- Listen to your teacher for special safety directions. If you don't understand something, ask for help.

During the Experiment

- Wear safety goggles when your teacher tells you to wear them and whenever you see ⌀.
- Wear a safety apron if you work with anything messy or anything that might spill.
- If you spill something, wipe it up right away or ask your teacher for help.
- Tell your teacher if something breaks. If glass breaks do not clean it up yourself.
- Keep your hair and clothes away from open flames. Tie back long hair and roll up long sleeves.
- Be careful around a hot plate. Know when it is on and when it is off. Remember that the plate stays hot for a few minutes after you turn it off.
- Keep your hands dry around electrical equipment.
- Don't eat or drink anything during the experiment.

After the Experiment

- Put equipment back the way your teacher tells you.
- Dispose of things the way your teacher tells you.
- Clean up your work area and wash your hands.

In the Field

- Always be accompanied by a trusted adult—like your teacher or a parent or guardian.
- Never touch animals or plants without the adult's approval. The animal might bite. The plant might be poison ivy or another dangerous plant.

Responsibility

Acting safely is one way to be responsible. You can also be responsible by treating animals, the environment, and each other with respect in the class and in the field.

Treat Living Things with Respect

- If you have animals in the classroom, keep their homes clean. Change the water in fish tanks and clean out cages.
- Feed classroom animals the right amounts of food.
- Give your classroom animals enough space.
- When you observe animals, don't hurt them or disturb their homes.
- Find a way to care for animals while school is on vacation.

Treat the Environment with Respect

- Do not pick flowers.
- Do not litter, including gum and food.
- If you see litter, ask your teacher if you can pick it up.
- Recycle materials used in experiments. Ask your teacher what materials can be recycled instead of thrown away. These might include plastics, aluminum, and newspapers.

Treat Each Other with Respect

- Use materials carefully around others so that people don't get hurt or get stains on their clothes.
- Be careful not to bump people when they are doing experiments. Do not disturb or damage their experiments.
- If you see that people are having trouble with an experiment, help them.

COLLECT DATA

Use a Hand Lens

You use a hand lens to magnify an object, or make the object look larger. With a hand lens, you can see details that would be hard to see without the hand lens.

Magnify a Piece of Cereal

1. Place a piece of your favorite cereal on a flat surface. Look at the cereal carefully. Draw a picture of it.
2. Hold the hand lens so that it is just above the cereal. Look through the lens, and slowly move it away from the cereal. The cereal will look larger.
3. Keep moving the hand lens until the cereal begins to look blurry. Then move the lens a little closer to the cereal until you can see it clearly.
4. Draw a picture of the cereal as you see it through the hand lens. Fill in details that you did not see before.
5. Repeat this activity using objects you are studying in science. It might be a rock, some soil, a flower, a seed, or something else.

Use a Microscope

Hand lenses make objects look several times larger. A microscope, however, can magnify an object to look hundreds of times larger.

Examine Salt Grains

1. Place the microscope on a flat surface. Always carry a microscope with both hands. Hold the arm with one hand, and put your other hand beneath the base.
2. Look at the drawing to learn the different parts of the microscope.
3. Move the mirror so that it reflects light up toward the stage. Never point the mirror directly at the Sun or a bright light.
4. Place a few grains of salt on the slide. Put the slide under the stage clips on the stage. Be sure that the salt grains are over the hole in the stage.
5. Look through the eyepiece. Turn the focusing knob slowly until the salt grains come into focus.
6. Draw what the grains look like through the microscope.
7. Look at other objects through the microscope. Try a piece of leaf, a strand of human hair, or a pencil mark.

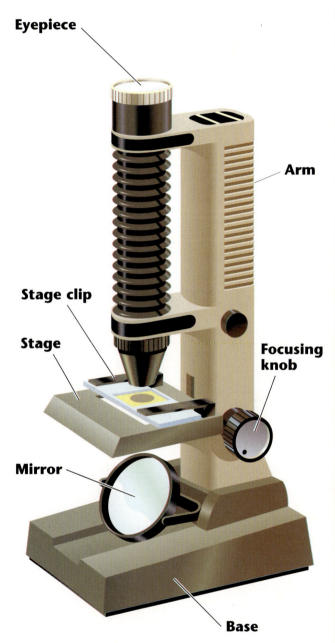

COLLECT DATA

Use a Compass

You use a compass to find directions. A compass is a small, thin magnet that swings freely, like a spinner in a board game. One end of the magnet always points north. This end is the magnet's north pole. How does a compass work?

1. Place the compass on a surface that is not made of magnetic material. A wooden table or a sidewalk works well.
2. Find the magnet's north pole. The north pole is marked in some way, usually with a color or an arrowhead.
3. Notice the letters *N, E, S,* and *W* on the compass. These letters stand for the directions north, east, south, and west. When the magnet stops swinging, turn the compass so that the *N* lines up with the north pole of the magnet.
4. Face to the north. Then face to the east, to the south, and to the west.
5. Repeat this activity by holding the compass in your hand and then at different places indoors and outdoors.

Use a Telescope

A telescope makes faraway objects, like the Moon, look larger. A telescope also lets you see stars that are too faint to see with just your eyes.

Look at the Moon

1. Look at the Moon in the night sky. Draw a picture of what you see. Draw as many details as you can.
2. Point a telescope toward the Moon. Look through the eyepiece of the telescope. Move the telescope until you see the Moon. Turn the knob until the Moon comes into focus.
3. Draw a picture of what you see. Include details. Compare your two pictures.

Look at the Stars

1. Find the brightest star in the sky. Notice if there are any other stars near it.
2. Point a telescope toward the brightest star. Look through the eyepiece and turn the knob until the stars come into focus. Move the telescope until you find the brightest star.
3. Can you see stars through the telescope that you cannot see with just your eyes?

COLLECT DATA

Use a Camera, Tape Recorder, Map, and Compass

Camera

You can use a camera to record what you observe in nature. Keep these tips in mind.

1. Hold the camera steady. Gently press the button so that you do not jerk the camera.
2. Try to take pictures with the Sun at your back. Then your pictures will be bright and clear.
3. Don't get too close to the subject. Without a special lens, the picture could turn out blurry.
4. Be patient. If you are taking a picture of an animal, you may have to wait for the animal to appear.

Tape Recorder

You can record observations on a tape recorder. This is sometimes better than writing notes because a tape recorder can record your observations at the exact time you are making them. Later you can listen to the tape and write down your observations.

Map and Compass

When you are busy observing nature, it might be easy to get lost. You can use a map of the area and a compass to find your way. Here are some tips.

1. Lightly mark on the map your starting place. It might be the place where the bus parked.
2. Always know where you are on the map compared to your starting place. Watch for landmarks on the map, such as a river, a pond, trails, or buildings.
3. Use the map and compass to find special places to observe, such as a pond. Look at the map to see which direction the place is from you. Hold the compass to see where that direction is.
4. Use your map and compass with a friend.

MAKE MEASUREMENTS

Length

Find Length with a Ruler

1. Look at this section of a ruler. Each centimeter is divided into 10 millimeters. How long is the paper clip?
2. The length of the paper clip is 3 centimeters plus 2 millimeters. You can write this length as 3.2 centimeters.
3. Place the ruler on your desk. Lay a pencil against the ruler so that one end of the pencil lines up with the left edge of the ruler. Record the length of the pencil.
4. Trade your pencil with a classmate. Measure and record the length of each other's pencils. Compare your answers.

Measuring Area

Area is the amount of surface something covers. To find the area of a rectangle, multiply the rectangle's length by its width. For example, the rectangle here is 3 centimeters long and 2 centimeters wide. Its area is 3 cm x 2 cm = 6 square centimeters. You write the area as 6 cm^2.

1. Find the area of your science book. Measure the book's length to the nearest centimeter. Measure its width.
2. Multiply the book's length by its width. Remember to put the answer in cm^2.

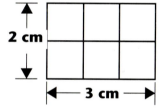

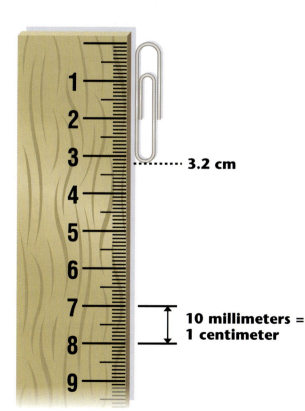

MAKE MEASUREMENTS

Time

You use timing devices to measure how long something takes to happen. Some timing devices you use in science are a clock with a second hand and a stopwatch. Which one is more accurate?

Comparing a Clock and a Stopwatch

1. Look at a clock with a second hand. The second hand is the hand that you can see moving. It measures seconds.
2. Get an egg timer with falling sand or some device like a windup toy that runs down after a certain length of time. When the second hand of the clock points to 12, tell your partner to start the egg timer. Watch the clock while the sand in the egg timer is falling.
3. When the sand stops falling, count how many seconds it took. Record this measurement. Repeat the activity, and compare the two measurements.
4. Switch roles with your partner.
5. Look at a stopwatch. Click the button on the top right. This starts the time. Click the button again. This stops the time. Click the button on the top left. This sets the stopwatch back to zero. Notice that the stopwatch tells time in hours, minutes, seconds, and hundredths of a second.
6. Repeat the activity in steps 1–3, but use the stopwatch instead of a clock. Make sure the stopwatch is set to zero. Click the top right button to start timing.

Click the button again when the sand stops falling. Make sure you and your partner time the sand twice.

0 minutes   25 seconds   72 hundredths of a second

More About Time

1. Use the stopwatch to time how long it takes an ice cube to melt under cold running water. How long does an ice cube take to melt under warm running water?
2. Match each of these times with the action you think took that amount of time.

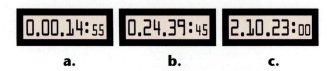

a.   b.   c.

1. A Little League baseball game
2. Saying the Pledge of Allegiance
3. Recess

R12

Volume

Have you ever used a measuring cup? Measuring cups measure the volume of liquids. Volume is the amount of space something takes up. To bake a cake, you might measure the volume of water, vegetable oil, or melted butter. In science you use special measuring cups called beakers and graduated cylinders. These containers are marked in milliliters (mL).

Measure the Volume of a Liquid

1. Look at the beaker and at the graduated cylinder. The beaker has marks for each 25 mL up to 200 mL. The graduated cylinder has marks for each 1 mL up to 100 mL.
2. The surface of the water in the graduated cylinder curves up at the sides. You measure the volume by reading the height of the water at the flat part. What is the volume of water in the graduated cylinder? How much water is in the beaker? They both contain 75 mL of water.
3. Pour 50 mL of water from a pitcher into a graduated cylinder. The water should be at the 50-mL mark on the graduated cylinder. If you go over the mark, pour a little water back into the pitcher.
4. Pour the 50 mL of water into a beaker.
5. Repeat steps 3 and 4 using 30 mL, 45 mL, and 25 mL of water.
6. Measure the volume of water you have in the beaker. Do you have about the same amount of water as your classmates?

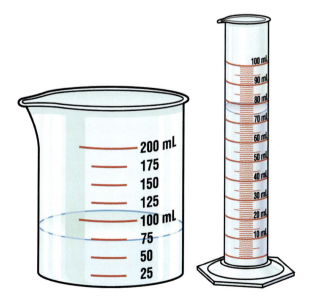

MAKE MEASUREMENTS

Mass

Mass is the amount of matter an object has. You use a balance to measure mass. To find the mass of an object, you balance it with objects whose masses you know. Let's find the mass of a box of crayons.

Measure the Mass of a Box of Crayons

1. Place the balance on a flat, level surface. Check that the two pans are empty and clean.
2. Make sure the empty pans are balanced with each other. The pointer should point to the middle mark. If it does not, move the slider a little to the right or left to balance the pans.
3. Gently place a box of crayons on the left pan. The pan will drop lower.
4. Add masses to the right pan until the pans are balanced. You can use paper clips.
5. Count the number of paper clips that are in the right pan. Two paper clips equal about one gram. What is the mass of the box of crayons? Record the number. After the number, write a *g* for "grams."

Predict the Mass of More Crayons

1. Leave the box of crayons and the masses on the balance.
2. Get two more crayons. If you put them in the pan with the box of crayons, what do you think the mass of all the crayons will be? Write down what you predict the total mass will be.
3. Check your prediction. Gently place the two crayons in the left pan. Add masses, such as paper clips, to the right pan until the pans are balanced.
4. Calculate the mass as you did before. Record this number. How close is it to your prediction?

More About Mass

What was the mass of all your crayons? It was probably less than 100 grams. What would happen if you replaced the crayons with a pineapple? You may not have enough masses to balance the pineapple. It has a mass of about 1,000 grams. That's the same as 1 kilogram because *kilo* means "1,000."

MAKE MEASUREMENTS

Weight/Force

You use a spring scale to measure weight. An object has weight because the force of gravity pulls down on the object. Therefore, weight is a force. Like all forces weight is measured in newtons (N).

Measure the Weight of an Object

1. Look at your spring scale to see how many newtons it measures. See how the measurements are divided. The spring scale shown here measures up to 10 N. It has a mark for every 1 N.
2. Hold the spring scale by the top loop. Put the object to be measured on the bottom hook. If the object will not stay on the hook, place it in a net bag. Then hang the bag from the hook.
3. Let go of the object slowly. It will pull down on a spring inside the scale. The spring is connected to a pointer. The pointer on the spring scale shown here is a small bar.
4. Wait for the pointer to stop moving. Read the number of newtons next to the pointer. This is the object's weight. The mug in the picture weighs 3 N.

More About Spring Scales

You probably weigh yourself by standing on a bathroom scale. This is a spring scale. The force of your body stretches or presses a spring inside the scale. The dial on the scale is probably marked in pounds—the English unit of weight. One pound is equal to about 4.5 newtons.

Here are some spring scales you may have seen.

Temperature

Temperature is how hot or cold something is. You use a thermometer to measure temperature. A thermometer is made of a thin tube with colored liquid inside. When the liquid gets warmer, it expands and moves up the tube. When the liquid gets cooler, it contracts and moves down the tube. You may have seen most temperatures measured in degrees Fahrenheit (°F). Scientists measure temperature in degrees Celsius (°C).

Read a Thermometer

1. Look at the thermometer shown here. It has two scales—a Fahrenheit scale and a Celsius scale. Every 20 degrees on each scale has a number.
2. What is the temperature shown on the thermometer? At what temperature does water freeze? Give your answers in °F and in °C.

How Is Temperature Measured?

1. Fill a large beaker about one-half full of cool water. Find the temperature of the water by holding a thermometer in the water. Do not let the bulb at the bottom of the thermometer touch the sides or bottom of the beaker.
2. Keep the thermometer in the water until the liquid in the tube stops moving—about a minute. Read and record the temperature on the Celsius scale.
3. Fill another large beaker one-half full of warm water from a faucet. Be careful not to burn yourself by using hot water.
4. Find and record the temperature of the warm water just as you did in steps 1 and 2.

MAKE OBSERVATIONS

Weather

What was the weather like yesterday? What is it like today? The weather changes from day to day. You can observe different parts of the weather to find out how it changes.

Measure Temperature

1. Use a thermometer to find the air temperature outside. Look at page R17 to review thermometers.
2. Hold a thermometer outside for two minutes. Then read and record the temperature.
3. Take the temperature at the same time each day for a week. Record it in a chart.

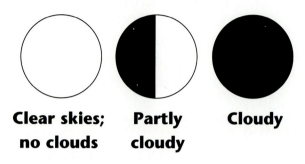

Clear skies; no clouds **Partly cloudy** **Cloudy**

2. Record in your chart if it is raining or snowing.
3. At the end of the week, how has the weather changed from day to day?

Observe Wind Speed and Direction

1. Observe how the wind is affecting things around you. Look at a flag or the branches of a tree. How hard is the wind blowing the flag or branches? Observe for about five minutes. Write down your observations.
2. Hold a compass to see which direction the wind is coming from. Write down this direction.
3. Observe the wind each day for a week. Record your observations in your chart.

Observe Clouds, Rain, and Snow

1. Observe how much of the sky is covered by clouds. Use these symbols to record the cloud cover in your chart each day.

Systems

What do a toy car, a tomato plant, and a yo-yo have in common? They are all systems. A system is a set of parts that work together to form a whole. Look at the three systems below. Think of how each part helps the system work.

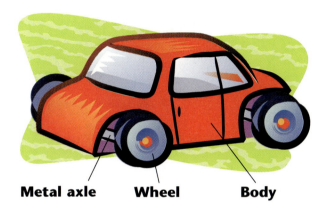

Metal axle   Wheel   Body

This system has three main parts—the body, the axles, and the wheels. Would the system work well if the axles could not turn?

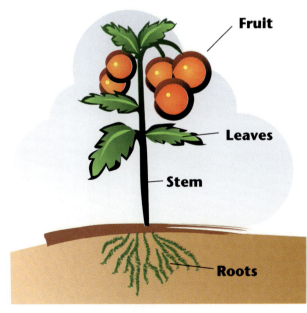

Fruit
Leaves
Stem
Roots

In this system roots take in water, and leaves make food. The stem carries water and food to different parts of the plant. What would happen if you cut off all the leaves?

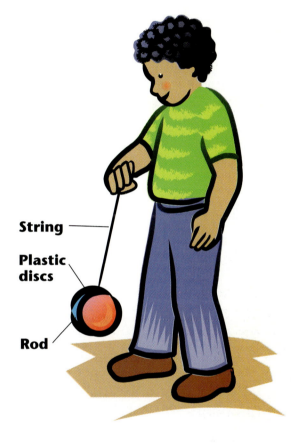

String
Plastic discs
Rod

Even simple things can be systems. How do all the parts of the yo-yo work together to make the toy go up and down?

Look for some other systems at school, at home, and outside. Remember to look for things that are made of parts. List the parts. Then describe how you think each part helps the system work.

R19

REPRESENT DATA
Make Graphs to Organize Data

When you do an experiment in science, you collect information. To find out what your information means, you can organize it into graphs. There are many kinds of graphs.

Bar Graphs

A bar graph uses bars to show information. For example, suppose you are growing a plant. Every week you measure how high the plant has grown. Here is what you find.

Week	Height (cm)
1	1
2	3
3	6
4	10
5	17
6	20
7	22
8	23

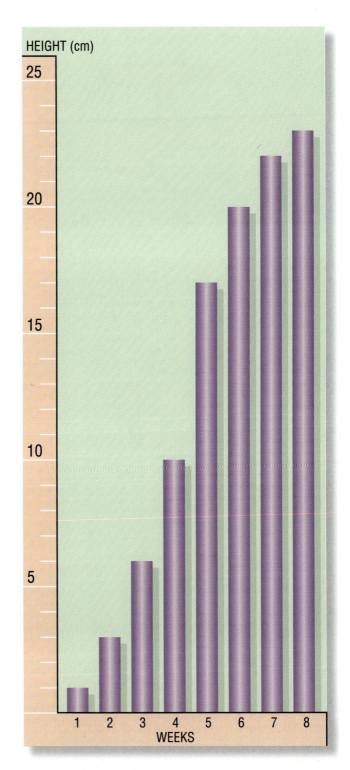

The bar graph at right organizes the measurements you collected so that you can easily compare them.

1. Look at the bar for week 2. Put your finger at the top of the bar. Move your finger straight over to the left to find how many centimeters the plant grew by the end of week 2.
2. Between which two weeks did the plant grow most?
3. When did plant growth begin to level off?

R20

Pictographs

A pictograph uses symbols, or pictures, to show information. Suppose you collect information about how much water your family uses each day. Here is what you find.

Activity	Water Used Each Day (L)
Drinking	10
Showering	180
Bathing	240
Brushing teeth	80
Washing dishes	140
Washing hands	30
Washing clothes	280
Flushing toilet	90

You can organize this information into the pictograph shown here. The pictograph has to explain what the symbol on the graph means. In this case, each bottle means 20 liters of water. A half bottle means half of 20, or 10 liters of water.

1. Which activity uses the most water?
2. Which activity uses the least water?

Make a Graph

Suppose you do an experiment to find out how far a toy car rolls on different surfaces. The results of your experiment are shown below.

Surface	Distance Car Rolled (cm)
Wood Floor	525
Sidewalk	325
Carpet Floor	150
Tile Floor	560
Grass	55

1. Decide what kind of graph would best show these results.
2. Make your graph.

A Family's Daily Use of Water

= 20 liters of water

REPRESENT DATA

Make Maps to Show Information

Locate Places

A map is a drawing that shows an area from above. Most maps have numbers and letters along the top and side. They help you find places easily. For example, what if you wanted to find the library on the map below. It is located at D7. Place a finger on the letter D along the side of the map and another finger on the number 7 at the top. Then move your fingers straight across and down the map until they meet. The library is located where D and 7 meet, or very nearby.

1. What building is located at G3?
2. The hospital is located three blocks south and three blocks east of the library. What is its number and letter?
3. Make a map of an area in your community. It might be a park or the area between your home and school. Include numbers and letters along the top and side. Use a compass to find north, and mark north on your map. Exchange maps with classmates.

Idea Maps

The map below left shows how places are connected to each other. Idea maps, on the other hand, show how ideas are connected to each other. Idea maps help you organize information about a topic.

Look at the idea map below. It connects ideas about water. This map shows that Earth's water is either fresh water or salt water. The map also shows four sources of fresh water. You can see that there is no connection between "rivers" and "salt water" on the map. This reminds you that salt water does not flow in rivers.

Make an idea map about a topic you are learning in science. Your map can include words, phrases, or even sentences. Arrange your map in a way that makes sense to you and helps you understand the ideas.

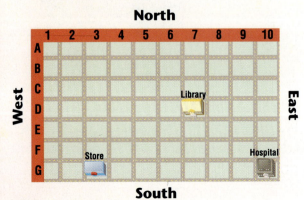

Make Tables and Charts to Organize Data

Tables help you organize data during experiments. Most tables have columns that run up and down, and rows that run across. The columns and rows have headings that tell you what kind of data goes in each part of the table.

A Sample Table

What if you are going to do an experiment to find out how long different kinds of seeds take to sprout? Before you begin the experiment, you should set up your table. Follow these steps.

1. In this experiment you will plant 20 radish seeds, 20 bean seeds, and 20 corn seeds. Your table must show how many of each kind of seed sprouted on days 1, 2, 3, 4, and 5.
2. Make your table with columns, rows, and headings. You might use a computer. Some computer programs let you build a table with just the click of a mouse. You can delete or add columns and rows if you need to.
3. Give your table a title. Your table could look like the one here.

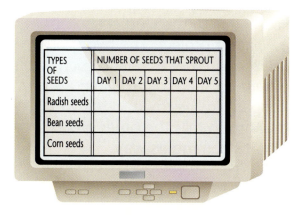

Make a Table

Now what if you are going to do an experiment to find out how temperature affects the sprouting of seeds? You will plant 20 bean seeds in each of two trays. You will keep each tray at a different temperature, as shown below, and observe the trays for seven days. Make a table that you can use for this experiment.

Make a Chart

A chart is simply a table with pictures as well as words to label the rows or columns.

R23

USE TECHNOLOGY
Computer

A computer has many uses. The Internet connects your computer to many other computers around the world, so you can collect all kinds of information. You can use a computer to show this information and write reports. Best of all you can use a computer to explore, discover, and learn.

You can also get information from CD-ROMs. They are computer disks that can hold large amounts of information. You can fit a whole encyclopedia on one CD-ROM.

Use Computers for a Project

Here is how one group of students uses computers as they work on a weather project.

1. The students use instruments to measure temperature, wind speed, wind direction, and other parts of the weather. They input this information, or data, into the computer. The students keep the data in a table. This helps them compare the data from one day to the next.

2. The teacher finds out that another group of students in a town 200 kilometers to the west is also doing a weather project. The two groups use the Internet to talk to each other and share data. When a storm happens in the town to the west, that group tells the other group that it's coming its way.

4. Meanwhile some students go to the library to gather more information from a CD-ROM disk. The CD-ROM has an encyclopedia that includes movie clips with sound. The clips give examples of different kinds of storms.

5. The students have kept all their information in a folder called Weather Project. Now they use that information to write a report about the weather. On the computer they can move paragraphs, add words, take out words, put in diagrams, and draw their own weather maps. Then they print the report in color.

3. The students want to find out more. They decide to stay on the Internet and send questions to a local TV weather forecaster. She has a Web site and answers questions from students every day.

USE TECHNOLOGY

Calculator

Sometimes after you make measurements, you have to add or subtract your numbers. A calculator helps you do this.

Add and Subtract Rainfall Amounts

The table shows the amount of rain that fell in a town each week during the summer. The amounts are given in centimeters (cm). Use a calculator to find the total amount of rain that fell during the summer.

Week	Rain (cm)
1	3
2	5
3	2
4	0
5	1
6	6
7	4
8	0
9	2
10	2
11	6
12	5

1. Make sure the calculator is on. Press the **ON** key.
2. To add the numbers, enter a number and press **+**. Repeat until you enter the last number. Then press **=**. You do not have to enter the zeroes. Your total should be 36.
3. Suppose you found out that you made a mistake in your measurements. Week 1 should be 2 cm less, Week 6 should be 3 cm less, Week 11 should be 1 cm less, and Week 12 should be 2 cm less. Subtract these numbers from your total. You should have 36 displayed on the calculator. Press **−** and enter the first number you want to subtract. Repeat until you enter the last number. Then press **=**. Compare your new total to your classmates' new totals.

R26

GLOSSARY

This Glossary will help you to pronounce and understand the meanings of the Science Words introduced in this book. The page number at the end of the definition tells where the word appears.

A

adaptation (ad′əp tā′shən) A characteristic that helps an organism survive in its environment. (p. 364)

antibody (an′ti bod′ē) A chemical made by the immune system to fight a particular disease. (p. 401)

asteroid (as′tə roid′) A small chunk of rock or metal that orbits the Sun. (p. 250)

atmosphere (at′məs fîr′) A layer of gases surrounding a planet. (p. 238)

axis (ak′sis) A real or imaginary line through the center of a spinning object. (p. 197)

B

bacteria (bak tîr′ē ə) One-celled living things. (p. 399)

PRONUNCIATION KEY

a	at	e	end	o	hot	u	up	hw	white	ə about
ā	ape	ē	me	ō	old	ū	use	ng	song	taken
ä	far	i	it	ô	fork	ü	rule	th	thin	pencil
âr	care	ī	ice	oi	oil	u̇	pull	th	this	lemon
		îr	pierce	ou	out	ûr	turn	zh	measure	circus

′ = primary accent; shows which syllable takes the main stress, such as **kil** in **kilogram** (kil′ə gram′)
′ = secondary accent; shows which syllables take lighter stresses, such as **gram** in **kilogram**

camouflage (kam′ə fläzh′) An adaptation that allows organisms to blend into their surroundings. (p. 366)

carbohydrate (kär′bō hī′drāt) A substance used by the body as its main source of energy. (p. 412)

carbon dioxide and oxygen cycle (kär′bən dī ok′sīd and ok′sə jən sī′kəl) The exchange of gases between producers and consumers. (p. 344)

cell (sel) 1. Tiny box-like part that is the basic building block of living things. (p. 56) 2. A source of electricity. (p. 184)

cell membrane (sel mem′brān) A thin outer covering of plant and animal cells. (p. 57)

circuit (sûr′kit) The path electricity flows through. (p. 184)

comet (kom′it) A body of ice and rock that orbits the Sun. (p. 250)

communicate (kə mū′ni kāt′) To share information by sending, receiving, and responding to signals. (p. 8)

community (kə mū′ni tē) All the living things in an ecosystem. (p. 324)

competition (kom′pi tish′ən) When one organism works against another to get what it needs to live. (p. 356)

compound (kom′pound) Two or more elements put together. (p. 158)

compound machine (kom′pound mə shēn′) Two or more simple machines put together. (p. 122)

conifer (kon′ə fər) A tree that produces seeds inside of cones. (p. 35)

consumer (kən sü′mər) An organism that eats producers or other consumers. (p. 334)

corona (kə rō′nə) The outermost layer of gases surrounding the Sun. (p. 229)

crater (krā′tər) A hollow area in the ground. (p. 208)

cytoplasm (sī′tə plaz′əm) A clear, jelly-like material that fills plant and animal cells. (p. 57)

D

data (dā′tə) Information. (p. 82)

decomposer (dē′kəm pō′zər) An organism that breaks down dead plant and animal material. (p. 336)

degree (di grē′) The unit of measurement for temperature. (p. 166)

dermis (dûr′mis) The layer of skin just below the epidermis. (p. 390)

development (di vel′əp mənt) The way a living thing changes during its life. (p. 4)

digestion (di jes′chən) The process of breaking down food. (p. 422)

E

earthquake (ûrth′kwāk′) A sudden movement in the rocks that make up Earth's crust. (p. 282)

eclipse (i klips′) When one object passes into the shadow of another object. (p. 218)

ecosystem (ek′ō sis′təm) All the living and nonliving things in an environment. (p. 324)

element (el′ə mənt) A building block of matter. (p. 157)

PRONUNCIATION KEY

a at; ā ape; ä far; âr care; e end; ē me; i it; ī ice; îr pierce; o hot; ō old; ô fork; oi oil; ou out; u up; ū use; ü rule; ů pull; ûr turn; hw white; ng song; th thin; <u>th</u> this; zh measure; ə about, taken, pencil, lemon, circus

embryo (em′brē ō) A young organism that is just beginning to grow. (p. 34)

endangered (en dān′jərd) In danger of becoming extinct. (p. 378)

energy (en′ər jē) The ability to do work. (p. 14, 101)

energy pyramid (en′ər jē pir′ə mid′) A diagram that shows how energy is used in an ecosystem. (p. 339)

environment (en vī′rən mənt) The things that make up an area, such as the land, water, and air. (p. 6)

epidermis (ep′ə dûr′mis) The outer layer of skin. (p. 388)

erosion (i rō′zhən) The process that occurs when weathered materials are carried away. (p. 272)

extinct (ek stingkt′) When there are no more of a certain plant or animal. (p. 378)

F

fats (fatz) Substances used by the body as long-lasting sources of energy. (p. 413)

fertilizer (fûr′tə lī′zər) A substance used to keep plants healthy. (p. 311)

fiber (fī′bər) Material that helps move wastes through the body. (p. 414)

flowering plant (flou′ər ing plant) A plant that produces seeds inside of flowers. (p. 35)

food chain (füd chān) A series of organisms that depend on one another for food. (p. 334)

food web • hurricane

food web (füd web) Several food chains that are connected. (p. 338)

force (fôrs) A push or pull. (p. 78)

friction (frik′shən) A force that occurs when one object rubs against another. (p. 90)

fuel (fū′əl) Something burned to provide heat or power. (p. 230)

G

gas (gas) Matter that has no definite shape or volume. (p. 142)

germinate (jûr′mə nāt) To begin growing. (p. 34)

glacier (glā′shər) A large mass of ice in motion. (p. 272)

gland (gland) A part of the body that makes substances the body needs. (p. 389)

gravity (grav′i tē) The pulling force between two objects. (p. 80)

H

habitat (hab′i tat′) The place where a plant or animal naturally lives and grows. (p. 324)

heat (hēt) A form of energy that makes things warmer. (p. 166)

helper T-cells (hel′pər tē selz) White blood cells that send signals to warn that germs have invaded the body. (p. 401)

hibernate (hī′bər nāt′) To rest or sleep through the cold winter. (p. 18)

host (hōst) The organism a parasite lives in or on. (p. 347)

hurricane (hûr′i kān′) A violent storm with strong winds and heavy rains. (p. 280)

PRONUNCIATION KEY

a at; ā ape; ä far; âr care; e end; ē me; i it; ī ice; îr pierce; o hot; ō old; ô fork; oi oil; ou out; u up; ū use; ü rule; ú pull; ûr turn; hw white; ng song; th thin; <u>th</u> this; zh measure; ə about, taken, pencil, lemon, circus

I

immune system (i mūn′ sis′təm) All the body parts and activities that fight diseases. (p. 403)

immunity (i mū′ni tē) The body's ability to fight diseases caused by germs. (p. 403)

inclined plane (in klīnd′ plān) A flat surface that is raised at one end. (p. 118)

inherited trait (in her′i təd trāt) A characteristic that comes from your parents. (p. 28)

insulator (in′sə lā′tər) A material that heat doesn't travel through easily. (p. 170)

L

landform (land′fôrm′) A feature on the surface of Earth. (p. 264)

large intestine (lärj in tes′tin) Part of the body that removes water from undigested food. (p. 425)

learned trait (lûrnd trāt) Something that you are taught or learn from experience. (p. 28)

lens (lenz) A curved piece of glass. (p. 240)

lever (lev′ər) A straight bar that moves on a fixed point. (p. 109)

life cycle (līf sī′kəl) All the stages in an organism's life. (p. 24)

liquid (lik′wid) Matter that has a definite volume, but not a definite shape. (p. 142)

lunar eclipse (lü′nər i klips′) When Earth's shadow blocks the Moon. (p. 219)

M

machine (mə shēn′) A tool that makes work easier to do. (p. 108)

magnetism (mag′ni tiz′əm) The property of an object that makes it attract iron. (p. 154)

mass (mas) How much matter is in an object. (p. 133)

matter (mat′ər) What makes up an object. (p. 80)

melanin (mel′ə nin) A substance that gives skin its color. (p. 388)

metal (met′əl) A shiny material found in the ground. (p. 154)

metamorphosis (met′ə môr′fə sis) A change in the body form of an organism. (p. 25)

migrate (mī′grāt) To move to another place. (p. 18)

mineral (min′ə rəl) A substance found in nature that is not a plant or an animal. (pp. 49, 260)

mixture (miks′chər) Different types of matter mixed together. (p. 147)

motion (mō′shən) A change of position. (p. 70)

N

natural resource (nach′ər əl rē′sôrs′) A material on Earth that is necessary or useful to people. (p. 292)

nerve cells (nûrv selz) Cells that carry messages to and from all parts of the body. (p. 390)

newton (nü′tən) The unit used to measure pushes and pulls. (p. 78)

niche (nich) The job or role an organism has in an ecosystem. (p. 358)

PRONUNCIATION KEY

a at; ā ape; ä far; âr care; e end; ē me; i it; ī ice; îr pierce; o hot; ō old; ô fork; oi oil; ou out; u up; ū use; ü rule; ù pull; ûr turn; hw white; ng song; th thin; th this; zh measure; ə about, taken, pencil, lemon, circus

nonrenewable resource (non′ri nü′ə bəl rē′sôrs′) A resource that cannot be reused or replaced in a useful amount of time. (p. 302)

nucleus (nü′klē əs) A main control center found in plant and animal cells. (p. 57)

nutrient (nüt′rē ənt) A substance that your body needs for energy and growth. (p. 412)

O

opaque (ō pāk′) Does not allow light to pass through. (p. 176)

orbit (ôr′bit) The path an object follows as it revolves. (p. 198)

organ (ôr′gən) A group of tissues that work together. (p. 58)

organism (ôr′gə niz′əm) A living thing. (p. 4)

oxygen (ok′sə jən) A gas that is in air and water. (p. 16)

P

parasite (par′ə sīt) An organism that lives in or on another organism. (p. 347)

perish (per′ish) To not survive. (p. 377)

phase (fāz) Apparent change in the Moon's shape. (p. 207)

plain (plān) A large area of land with few hills. (p. 264)

planet (plan′it) A satellite of the Sun. (p. 228)

plateau (pla tō′) A flat area of land that rises above the land that surrounds it. (p. 265)

pollution (pə lü′shən) What happens when harmful substances get into water, air, or land. (p. 310)

population (pop′yə lā′shən) All the members of a certain type of living thing in an area. (p. 324)

pore (pôr) A tiny opening in the skin. (p. 391)

position (pə zish′ən) The location of an object. (p. 68)

pound (pound) The unit used to measure force and weight in the English system of measurement. (p. 81)

predator (pred′ə tər) An animal that hunts other animals for food. (p. 356)

prey (prā) The animal a predator hunts. (p. 356)

producer (prə dü′sər) An organism that makes its own food. (p. 334)

property (prop′ər tē) A characteristic of something. (p. 135)

protein (prō′tēn) A substance that the body uses for growth and the repair of cells. (p. 413)

pulley (pu̇l′ē) A simple machine that uses a wheel and a rope. (p. 112)

R

recycle (rē sī′kəl) To treat something so it can be used again. (p. 314)

reduce (ri düs′) To make less of something. (p. 312)

reflect (ri flekt′) To bounce off a surface. (p. 177)

relocate (ri lō′kāt) To find a new home. (p. 377)

PRONUNCIATION KEY

a at; ā ape; ä far; âr care; e end; ē me; i it; ī ice; îr pierce; o hot; ō old; ô fork; oi oil; ou out; u up; ū use; ü rule; u̇ pull; ûr turn; hw white; ng song; th thin; <u>th</u> this; zh measure; ə about, taken, pencil, lemon, circus

GLOSSARY

renewable resource (ri nü′ə bəl rē′sôrs′) A resource that can be replaced or used over and over again. (p. 296)

reproduction (rē′prə duk′shən) The way organisms make new living things just like themselves. (p. 5)

respond (ri spond′) The way a living thing reacts to changes in its environment. (p. 6)

reuse (v., rē ūz′) To use something again. (p. 314)

revolve (ri volv′) To move in a circle around an object. (p. 198)

rotate (rō′tāt) To turn around. (p. 196)

S

saliva (sə lī′və) A liquid in your mouth that helps soften and break down food. (p. 423)

satellite (sat′ə līt′) An object that orbits another, larger object in space. (p. 206)

screw (skrü) An inclined plane wrapped into a spiral. (p. 120)

simple machine (sim′pəl mə shēn′) A machine with few or no moving parts. (p. 109)

small intestine (smôl in tes′tin) A tube-like part of your body where most digestion takes place. (p. 425)

solar eclipse (sō′lər i klips′) When the Moon's shadow blocks the Sun. (p. 218)

solar system (sō′lər sis′təm) The Sun and all the objects that orbit the Sun. (p. 236)

solid (sol′id) Matter that has a definite shape and volume. (p. 142)

solution (sə lü′shən) A type of mixture that has one or more types of matter spread evenly through another. (p. 148)

speed (spēd) How fast an object moves. (p. 71)

star (stär) A hot sphere of gases that gives off energy. (p. 228)

stomach (stum′ək) Part of your body that has walls made of strong muscles that squeeze and mash food. (p. 424)

sunspot (sun′spot′) A dark area on the Sun's surface. (p. 229)

switch (swich) Opens or closes an electric circuit. (p. 185)

system (sis′təm) A group of parts that work together. (p. 46)

T

taste buds (tāst budz) Thousands of cells on your tongue that send the signals for sweet, sour, bitter, and salty to your brain. (p. 423)

telescope (tel′ə skōp′) A tool that gathers light to make faraway objects appear closer. (p. 240)

temperature (tem′pər ə chər) A measure of how hot or cold something is. (p. 166)

tissue (tish′ü) A group of cells that are alike. (p. 58)

V

vaccine (vak′sēn) A medicine that causes the body to form antibodies against a certain disease. (p. 404)

valley (val′ē) An area of land lying between hills. (p. 264)

PRONUNCIATION KEY

a **at**; ā **ape**; ä **far**; âr **care**; e **end**; ē **me**; i **it**; ī **ice**; îr **pierce**; o **hot**; ō **old**; ô **fork**; oi **oil**; ou **out**; u **up**; ū **use**; ü **rule**; ủ **pull**; ûr **turn**; hw **white**; ng **song**; th **thin**; <u>th</u> **this**; zh **measure**; ə **about, taken, pencil, lemon, circus**

virus (vī′rəs) A tiny particle that can reproduce only inside a living cell. (p. 399)

vitamin (vīt′ə mən) A substance used by the body for growth. (p. 414)

volcano (vol kā′nō) An opening in the surface of Earth. Melted rock, gases, rock pieces, and dust are forced out of this opening. (p. 283)

volume (vol′ūm) How much space matter takes up. (p. 132)

W

weathering (we<u>th</u>′ər ing) The process that causes rocks to crumble, crack, and break. (p. 270)

wedge (wej) Two inclined planes placed back to back. (p. 119)

weight (wāt) The pull of gravity on an object. (p. 81)

wheel and axle (hwēl and ak′səl) A wheel that turns on a post. (p. 111)

white blood cells (hwīt blud selz) Cells in the blood that fight bacteria and viruses. (p. 400)

work (würk) When a force changes the motion of an object. (p. 100)

INDEX

A

Adaptation, 364–366, 368, 381
AIDS, 406–407
Air, 16, 210, 305
Aluminum, 156–157
Animals, 22-23*, 24–27, 28*–29, 46-50*, 51, 57, 323*, 330-331, 334, 342–343*, 344-348*, 349, 356–359, 362–363*, 364, 374–378*
Antibodies, 401–402*, 404, 408
Area, R2–R3, R11
Asteroids, 250, 253
Atmosphere, 238–239, 253
Ax, 119
Axis, 197–198, 201, 224, 236, 256
Axles, 111, 113, 125

B

Bacteria, 336, 399, 408, 426
Balance, R14–R15, R20–21
Bar graph, 82*, 304*
Basalt, 262
Bear, 26
Biceps, 84–85
Bird, 27
Birth, 24–27
Blood, 391
Body parts, 44–45*, 46–50*, 51, 54–55*, 56*-59
Body system, 58
Body temperature, 391
Bulbs, 38

C

Calculator, R26
Calendar, 212–213
Camera, R10
Camouflage, 366–367*, 381
Carbohydrates, 412, 429
Carbon dioxide, 210, 239, 344–345
Carbon dioxide and oxygen cycle, 344–345, 352
Carver, George Washington, 298–299
Cell, electrical, 183*–184, 189, 192
Cell membrane, 57, 61
Cells, 56*, 57–59, 61
Cellulose, 60
Cell wall, 57
Celsius scale, R2–R3, R17
Centimeter, R2–R3
Chalk, changing, 271*
Changes
  in ecosystems, 372–373*, 374–378*, 379
  in living things, 3*–4, 22–23*, 24–27, 28*–29
  in matter, 144–145, 150–151, 168–169*, 177
  in motion, 87*–89, 100
  in rocks, 269*–270
Charts, reading, 27, 71, 143, 177, 184, 313, 357, 364, 368, 416, R23
Chemicals, 270–271*
Chlorine, 158
Chloroplasts, 57
Circuits, 184–185*, 189
Classifying, 50*, 61, 63, 141*–142, 146
Cleaning water, 311*
Clock, R12
Closed circuit, 184
Coal, 230, 302–303
Comets, 250, 253
Communicating, 8, 42, 146*, 191
Community, 324, 328*, 350–352
Comparing the Sun and Moon, 231*
Compass, R8, R10
Competition, 354–355*, 356–358*, 359, 361, 381
Compost, 39
Compound machines, 122–123, 125
Compounds, 158–159, 162
Computer, R24–R25
Conglomerate, 262
Conifers, 35–36, 42
Conservation, 188, 308–309*, 310–311*, 312–315, 360-361
Consumers, 334, 337*, 344–345, 352
Contour farming, 266–267
Contraction, 169
Controlling electrical flow, 185
Controlling experiments, 178*
Copper, 156–157
Corona, 229, 231, 253
Craters, 208, 210, 224, 239
Cuttings, 38
Cytoplasm, 57, 61

* Indicates an activity related to this topic.

Day – Food

D

Day, 194–195*, 196
Death, 24
Decomposers, 336–337*, 352
Defining terms, 328*
Degrees, 166, 189, R2–R3
Dermis, 390–391, 408
Designing experiments, 45*, 63, 107*, 127, 141*, 191, 245*, 255, 279*, 319, 363*, 383, 387*, 431
Development, 4, 9, 24, 26–27, 36
Diagrams, reading, 4, 16, 35, 57, 70, 72, 79, 88, 102, 109, 136, 167, 189, 199, 206, 219, 230, 237, 263, 271, 283, 303, 325, 327, 335, 376, 389, 401, 423
Digestion, 409, 422*–427, 429
Digestive system, 426–427, 432
Disease, 381, 388–389, 396–397*, 398–402*, 403–405
Distance, 67*, 71, 217*, R2–R3
Dust bowl, 284

E

Earth, 104–105, 194–195*, 196–200*, 201, 206–211, 214–215*, 216–222, 227*–228, 234–235*, 236–241, 258–259*, 260–261*, 262–265, 268–269*, 270–271*, 272–273*, 274–275, 278–279*, 280, 282–285, 290–291*, 292–295*, 296–297
Earthquakes, 104–105, 282–283
Earth's surface, 264–265, 268–269*, 270–271*, 272–273*, 274–275, 278–279*, 280–281*, 282–285, 290–291*, 292–294, 296–297
  changes to, 268–269*, 278–279*, 280–281*, 282–283
Eclipse, 218–224
Ecosystems, 323*, 324–327, 328*–331, 336–337*, 338–339, 343*–344, 357, 358*–359, 368, 372–373*, 374–377, 378*–379
Eggs, 30–31
Electrical flow, 185*
Electricity, 182–183*, 184–185*, 186–189, 192
Elements, 157–159, 160–162
Embryo, 34, 42
Endangered species, 378*–379, 381
Energy, 14, 16, 42, 49, 101*–102, 104–105, 143, 145, 166, 168, 171, 172–173, 176–177, 180–181, 226–227*, 229–230, 233, 302, 304*, 336, 360–361, 412
Energy pyramid, 339
Energy survey, 304*
Energy transformation, 336
English system of measures, R2–R3
Environment, 6–7*, 8–9, 18, 19, 48, 274, 322–323*, 324–328*, 362–363*, 364–367*, 368–369
Epidermis, 389, 390, 397*, 408
Epiglottis, 428
Equal forces, 89
Erosion, 266–267, 272, 273*, 274–279*, 280–281*, 296
Esophagus, 424
Evaporation, 145
Expansion, 169
Experimenting, 7*
Experiments, 7*, 45*, 63, 64, 107*, 127, 141*, 178*, 191, 245*, 255, 279*, 319, 383, 387*, 431. *See also* Explore activities *and* Quick Labs.
Explore activities, 3*, 13*, 23*, 33*, 45*, 55*, 67*, 77*, 87*, 99*, 107*, 117*, 131*, 141*, 153*, 165*, 175*, 183*, 195*, 205*, 215*, 227*, 235*, 245*, 259*, 279*, 291*, 301*, 309*, 311*, 323*, 333*, 343*, 355*, 373*, 387*, 397*, 411*, 421*
Extinction, 378*–379, 381

F

Fahrenheit scale, R2–R3, R17
Fats, 411*– 413, 429
Fertilizers, 311
Fiber, 414, 429
Flashlight, 185*
Flowering plants, 35, 42
Food, 332–333*, 340–341, 344–345, 410–411*, 412–415*, 416–417, 418–419, 420–421*, 422*–428

R40 * Indicates an activity related to this topic.

Food chains, 334–335, 338, 352
Food pyramid, 416
Food webs, 338, 352
Forces, 77*–81, 86–87*, 88–92*, 93, 94, 100, 109–110, 112, 119, R3, R16
Forest community, 328*
Forming a hypothesis, 273*
Formulating a model, 402*
Fortified cereal, 155*
Freeze-dried foods, 418–419
Friction, 90–91, 92*, 93, 94–95, 102, 104–105, 171
Frog, 25, 30–31
Fuels, 230, 233, 253, 302
Fulcrum, 109–110*
Fungi, 336

G

Gases, 16, 49, 142–143, 145–146*, 147–149, 150–151, 157, 169*, 210, 230–231, 248, 249, 250, 283, 302, 305, 344–345
Germination, 34, 37, 42
Germs, 396–397*, 398–402*, 403–405, 424, 426
Gills, 16
Glaciers, 272
Gland, 389, 390, 408, 424
Global positioning system, 74–75
Gneiss, 263
Gold, 156–157
Gram, 134, R2–R3
Granite, 260, 263
Graphs, R20–R21
Gravity, 80–81, 82*, 83, 136–137, 210, 220

Great Dark Spot, 249
Great Red Spot, 246
Growth and change, 24–27, 28*, 29

H

Habitat, 324–329, 344–345, 374–378*
Halley's comet, 252
Hand lens, R6
Heat, 164–165*, 166–169*, 170–171, 189, 230, 238
Helper T-cells, 400
Hibernation, 18
HIV virus, 406–407
Homes, 330–331
Host, 347, 352
Hurricanes, 280–281*, 286–289
Hydrogen, 158

I

Ideas, using, 61, 63, 125, 127, 189, 191, 253, 255, 317, 319, 381, 383, 429, 431
Identifying properties, 367*
Immune system, 403–404, 407–408
Immunity, 403, 408
Immunodeficiency, 406–407
Inclined plane, 118, 120, 125
Inferring, 247*, 253, 255
Inherited traits, 28*, 42
Inner planets, 234–235*, 236–237
Insects, 45*–46
Insulators, 170, 189
Interpreting data, 82*, 127*, 415*, 429
Investigating

ecosystems, 373*
food, 333*, 411*, 421*
forces, 77*
heat, 165*
light, 175*, 183*
living things, 3*, 13*, 23*, 55*, 343*
mining, 301*
motion, 87*
night and day, 195*
planets, 235*
plants and animals, 323*, 355*
protection against disease, 397*
rocks, 259*, 269*
shape of the Moon, 205*
size of the Sun and Moon, 215*
soil, 291*
speed, 67*
Sun's energy, 227*
what organisms need, 13*
work, 99*, 117*
Iron, 155*, 158, 187*

J

Journal writing, 63, 127, 191, 255, 319, 383, 431
Jupiter, 83, 236–237, 244–245*, 246–247*

K

Kidneys, 16
Kilogram (kg), 134

L

Landforms, 264, 268, 283
Landslides, 282–283
Large intestine, 425–426, 429

Learned traits – Motion

Learned traits, 24, 42
Length, R2–R3, R11
Lenses, 240*
Levers, 109–110*, 113, 114–115, 125, 128
Life cycles, 24–27, 28*–29, 32–33*, 34–37*
Light, 37*, 174–175*, 176–177, 178*–179, 183*–184, 192, 230, 247
Light waves, 180–181
Limestone, 260, 262–263
Liquid, 16, 49, 140–141*, 142–143, 145–146*, 147, 148–149, 150–151, 157, 162, 168, 178*
Lists, identifying, 61, 125
Living things, 2–3*, 4–7*, 8–11, 13*–15*, 16–19, 22–23*, 24–28*, 29, 33*–37*, 38–45*, 46–50*, 51–55*, 56*, 57–61, 322–323*, 324–328*, 329–337, 342–343*, 344–348*, 349–352, 354–355*, 356–358*, 359–363*, 364–369
  changes in, 3*–4, 22–23*, 24–27, 28*–29
  competition of, 354–355*, 356–358*, 359–361
  environment of, 6–7*, 8–9, 18–19, 48, 274, 322–323*, 324–328*, 362–363*, 364–367*, 368–369
  features of, 4–5, 6–7*, 8–9
  life cycle of, 24–27, 28*–29, 32–33*, 34–37*
  needs of, 13*–15*, 16–19, 342–343*, 344–348*, 349
  parts of, 44–45*, 46–49, 50*–51, 54–55*, 56*, 57–59
  places to live, 322–323*, 324–328*, 329–337*
  recycling, 336–337
  roles for, 342–343*, 344–348*, 349–352
  survival of, 362–363*, 364–368*, 369

L

Length, R2–R3, R11
Lizards, 370–371
Load, 109–110, 112
Lunar calendar, 212–213
Lunar eclipse, 219, 222–224
Lungs, 16

M

Machines, 108–110*, 111–113, 116–117*, 118–121*, 122–125
Magnetism, 154, 162
Magnets, 152–153*, 154
Maps, 72, R10, R22
Marble, 263
Mars, 83, 236–237, 239, 242–243
Mass, 133, 134*, 135–136, 138–139, 210
  measuring, 134*, 136, 138–139, 295, R2–R3, R14–R15
Matter, 80–82*, 83, 132–133, 134*–137, 141*–146*, 147–153*, 168–169, 177
  building blocks of, 152–153*, 154–155*
  changes in, 144–145, 150–151, 168–169*, 177
  classifying, 141*–146*
  forms of, 140–141*, 142–143, 147–149
  gravity and, 80, 81–82*, 83
  heat and, 164–165*, 166–169*, 170–171, 230, 238
  properties of, 134*–135, 136–137, 140
Measurement, 134*, 136, 138–139, 295*, R2–R3
Melanin, 388–389, 408
Mercury, 236–237, 238
Metals, 154–155*, 156, 162
Metamorphosis, 25–26, 42
Meters, R2
Metric system, R2–R3
Microscope, 56*, R7
Migration, 18, 42
Millimeter, R2–R3
Minerals, 49, 61, 260–261*, 293, 414
Mineral scratch test, 261
Mining, 301*–302
Mixtures, 147–149, 158, 162
Models, making, 402*, 408
Monarch butterfly, 2–21, 24
Moon, 204–205*, 206–208, 209*, 210, 212–213, 214, 215*–216, 217*–222, 231*, 236–23, R9
Motion, 70–73, 86–87*, 88–92*, 93, 94, 99*, 100–101*, 102–103
  changes in, 87*–89, 100
  defining, 70–71
  forces in, 77*–81, 86–87*, 88–92*, 93, 94, 100, 109–110, 112, 119
  friction, 90–91, 92*, 93, 94–95, 102, 104–105, 171

R42   * Indicates an activity related to this topic.

of planets, 198, 206–207, 218, 224, 235–238, 239, 246, 248, 249, 250
Movement, 66–67*, 68–73, 86–87*, 88–92*, 93, 99*, 100–101*, 102–103, 235*–236
Moving parts, 46, 48
Moving things, 66–67*, 68–73
  position, 68–69*, 70–72
  speed, 67*, 71
Muscles, 84–85
Music machines, 114–115

N

Natural gas, 302, 304
Natural resources, 292–297, 300–301*, 302–304*, 305, 360–361
Nectar, 35
Neptune, 236–237, 249
Nerve cells, 390–391, 408
Nerves, 391
Newton, 78, 136, R3
Niche, 358*–359, 381
Night, 194–195*, 196
Nonrenewable resources, 302–303, 360–361
North pole, 197–198
Nucleus, 57, 61
Numbers, using, 121*
Nutrients, 34, 39, 412–415*, 416–417
Nutrition, 409, 415*
Nutrition label, 415

O

Objects, 130–131*, 132–134*, 136–137
Observations, making, 247*, 328*, 367*
Obsidian, 262
Oil, 230, 304
Opaque, 176, 189
Open circuit, 184
Orbit, 198, 206–207, 218, 224, 235–238, 239, 246, 248, 249, 250
Organ, 58, 61
Organisms, 4–5, 6–7*, 8–9, 12–13*, 14–19, 22–23*, 24–28*, 29, 44–45*, 46–50*, 51, 54–55*, 56*–59, 323*, 324–327, 328*–331, 336–337*, 338–339, 343*–344, 345–348*, 349, 357, 358*–359, 362–363*, 364–367*, 368–369, 372–373*, 374–377, 378*–379
  body parts of, 44–45*, 46–50*, 51, 54–55*, 56*–59
  changes in, 3*–4, 22–23*, 24–27, 28*–29
  decomposers, 336–337*
  ecosystems of, 323*, 324–327, 328*–331, 336–337*, 338–339, 343*–344, 357, 358*–359, 368, 372–373*, 374–377, 378*–379
  environment, 322–323*
  features of, 3*–7*, 8–9
  needs of, 13*–15*, 16–19, 342–343*, 344–348*, 349
  organization of, 58
  response of, 6–7*, 8–9, 17–18, 48
  survival characteristics, 362–363*, 364–367*, 368–369, 377–378*
Outer covering, 47
Oxygen, 16, 158, 210, 344–345

P

Parasite, 347, 352
Partial eclipse, 220
Parts of living things, 44–45*, 46–49, 50*–51, 54–55*, 56*–59
  parts of parts, 46
  parts that get information, 46, 48
  parts that move, 46, 48
  parts that protect and support, 46–47, 50*
  parts that take in materials, 46, 49
  smaller, 54–55*, 56*, 57–59
Patterns, using, 209*
Periodic table, 160–161
Perishing, 377–378
Phases, of the Moon, 206–207, 209*, 211, 224
Piano, 114–115
Plain, 264–265
Planetary rings, 246–249
Planets, 228, 234–235*, 236–239, 240*, 241–246, 247*, 248–251, 253
Plant life cycle, 33*–34, 36
Plants, 32–33*, 34–37*, 38–39, 40–41, 46, 52–53, 57, 60, 64, 323*, 330–331, 334, 342–343*, 344–348*, 349, 355*–359, 364–365, 374–375
Plastics, 306–307
Plateau, 265

Plow – Small intestine

Plow, 119
Pluto, 236–237, 249
Pollen, 35–36
Pollination, 35–36
Pollution, 308–309*, 310–311*, 312, 316
Pond ecosystem, 326
Population, 324, 344–347, 352
Pores, 391, 408
Position, 68–69*, 70–72
Pounds, 81, R2–R3
Predator, 356, 360–361, 373*, 381
Predicting, 63, 191, 209*, 255
Prey, 356, 373*, 381
Problems and puzzles, 42, 61, 64, 96, 125, 128, 162, 224, 253, 256, 288, 317, 320
Problem solving, 64, 128, 192, 256, 320, 384, 432
Producers, 334, 337*, 344–345, 352
Prominences, 231*
Properties, 135–137, 140–141*, 142–143, 147, 150–151, 153*, 154–155*, 158, 162, 175*, 294, 367*
Proteins, 413
Pulley, 112–113, 125, 128
Pulls, 76–77*, 78–81, 82*, 83, 109
Pushes, 76–77*, 78–81, 82*, 83, 109

Q

Quick Lab, 15*, 28*, 37*, 56*, 69*, 92*, 101*, 110*, 134*, 155*, 169*, 185*, 200*, 217*, 231*, 240*, 261*, 271*, 281*, 337*, 348*, 358*, 378*, 392*, 422*

R

Rabbits, 381
Radar, 288–289
Radiating, 220
Rain forest, 357
Ramp, 117*–118
Rate, R3
Recycling, 314–315, 336–337, R5
Reducing, 312
Reflection, 176–177, 189, 208
Refrigeration, 172–173
Relocation, 377–378
Renewable resources, 296, 300, 305
Reproduction, 5, 9, 24, 33*, 34–36, 38, 42, 348*, 365
Resource conservation, 308–309*, 310–315
Resources, 292–297, 300–301*, 302–304*, 305, 308–309*, 310–315, 360–361
Response of organisms, 6–7*, 8–9, 17–18, 48
Reuse, 314–315
Revolution, 198–199, 210, 224, 236, 239, 248
Rock climbing, 94–95
Rocks, 94–95, 259*–260, 261*–263, 269*, 270, 272–273*, 274–275, 290–291*
 changes in, 269*–270
 comparing, 259*–261*
 forming, 262–263
Rotation, 196, 210, 224, 236
Rust, 158

S

Safety rules, R4–R5
Saliva, 423
Sandstone, 262
Satellite, 206, 220, 224, 239
Saturn, 236–237, 248, 256
Schist, 263
Science Journal, 63, 127, 191, 255, 319, 383, 431. *See also* Explore Activities, Quick Lab, Skill Builders.
Screw, 120, 121*, 125
Seasons, 198
Seeds, 35–37*, 348*, 384
Seismic waves, 180–181
Serving size, 415
Shade, 37*
Shadow, 218–220
Shale, 262, 263
SI (International System) measures, R2–R3
Sign language, 14–15
Silver, 156
Simple machines, 108–109, 110*–113, 116–117*, 119–121*, 122–125
Skill builders, 7*, 50*, 82*, 121*, 146*, 178*, 209*, 247*, 273*, 295*, 328*, 367*, 402*, 415*
Skills, using, 7*, 50*, 61, 63, 82*, 125, 127, 146*, 178*, 189, 191, 209*, 247*, 253, 255, 273*, 295*, 317, 319, 328*, 367*, 381, 383, 429, 431
Skin, 386–387*, 388–391, 392*–395, 397*
Slate, 263
Small intestine, 425, 429

R44 * Indicates an activity related to this topic.

Sodium, 158
Sodium chloride, 158
Soil, 39, 165*, 266–267, 290–291*, 292–295*, 296, 384
   layers of, 293
   properties of, 294
Soil formation, 293
Solar cells, 233
Solar eclipse, 218, 220, 222–224
Solar energy, 360–361
Solar flare, 231
Solar storm, 231
Solar system, 236–240*, 244–245*, 246–247*, 248–251, 253, 256
Solar wind, 250
Solids, 16, 49, 140–141*, 142–143, 145–146*, 147, 150–151, 157, 162
Solution, 148, 162
Sound waves, 180–181
South pole, 197
Space, 131*–132, 137
Space foods, 418–419
Space probe, 238, 242–243, 256
Speed, 67*, 71
Sphere, 205*–206
Spores, 38
Spring scale, 77*–78, R16
Stars, 202–203, 228, 253
Star time, 202–203
Steel, 155*–156
Stomach, 424–425, 429
Stone symbols, 266–267
Stopwatch, R12
Subsoil, 293
Summarizing, 253, 429
Sun, 194–195*, 196–200*, 203, 208, 214, 215*–216, 217*–218, 220–223, 227*–233, 235*, 237*–239, 246, 249, 250, 394–395
Sundial, 199*
Sun's energy, 226–227*, 228, 229–231
Sunspots, 229, 231, 253
Survey, 304*
Survival, 362–363*, 364–367*, 368–369, 377–378*
Switch, electrical, 185, 189
System, R19
   electrical, 184
Systems of living things, 46, 61

T

Tables, making, 50*, 146*, R23
Tape recorder, R10
Taste buds, 423, 429
Technology in science, 74–75, 172–173, 288–289
Telescope, 240*–241, 253, R9
Temperate forest, 357
Temperature, 166, 227*–228, 281*, 391, R2–R3, R17–R18
Terrace farming, 266–267
Thermometer, 166, 168
Tilted axis, 197–198, 201, 248, 256
Time, 67*, 71, 202–203, 212–213
Tissue, 58, 61
Topsoil, 293
Total eclipse, 220
Trash, 313–314
Triceps, 84–85
Tubers, 38

U

Ultraviolet light, 394–395
Unbalanced forces, 89
Unequal forces, 89
Uranus, 236–237, 248
Using numbers, 121*
Using observations, 247
Using patterns, 209*
Using variables, 178*

V

Vaccines, 404, 408
Valley, 264–265
Variables, using, 178*, 189
Venus, 236–237, 238
Viruses, 381, 399, 406–408
Vitamins, 414, 429
Volcanic eruption, 372
Volcanoes, 239, 283
Volume, 131*–132, 133, 135, 245*–246, 295*, R2–R3, R13

W

Wastes, 15*, 16, 49, 391, 425
Water, 15*, 158, 165*, 210, 295*, 305, 308–309*, 310–311*, 360–361, 414
Water filtration model, 311*
Water pollution, 308–309*, 310–311*, 316
Water transport system, 58
Water vapor, 145
Weather, 281
Weathering, 270, 272, 273*–275, 278–279*, 280–281*
Weather satellites, 288–289
Wedge, 119, 125

Weight – Year

Weight, 81, 82*, 83, 136, R2–R3, R16
Wheels, 111–113, 125
White blood cells, 400, 403, 408
Wind energy, 360–361
Windpipe, 428
Work, 98–99*, 100–101*, 106–107*, 108, 110*, 111–113, 116–117*, 118–121*, 122–123, 125

Y

Year, 198

* Indicates an activity related to this topic.

CREDITS

Design & Production: Kirchoff/Wohlberg, Inc.

Maps: Geosystems.

Transvision: Ken Karp (photography); Michael Maydak (illustration).

Illustrations: Ken Batelman p.428; Ka Botzis: pp. 271, 274, 293, 325, 368, 376; Elizabeth Callen: 360; Barbara Cousins: pp. 85, 423, 424, 425; Steve Cowden pp. 350–351; Marie Dauenheimer: pp. 388–389, 390–391, 399, 400–401; Michael DiGiorgio: pp. 328, 335, 339, 364; Jeff Fagan: pp. 12, 58, 88, 89, 91, 101, 102; Lee Glynn: pp. 15, 71, 72, 82, 83, 136, 159, 230, 256, 313, 352, 357, 384, 398, 416, 432; Kristen Goeters: p. 137; Colin Hayes: p. 173 Handbook pp. R7, R11, R13, R20–R23; Nathan Jarvis: pp. 68, 69, 70; Matt Kania: pp. 264, 283; Virge Kask: pp. 14, 26–27; Fiona King: 222, 223. Tom Leonard: pp. 16, 57, 81, 90, 196, 197, 200, 208, 236–237; Olivia: Handbook pp. R2–R4, R9, R10, R13, R16–R19, R21, R23–R25; Sharron O'Neil: pp. 4, 34, 35, 36, 40, 60, 64, 288, 303, 317, 320; Pat Rasch: pp. 79, 80, 118, 119, 120, 121, 128; Rob Schuster: pp. 115, 185, 186, 192, 198–199, 206–207, 216, 218, 219, 244; Casey Shain: p. 304; Wendy Smith: pp. 338, 344, 326–327; Matt Straub: pp. 42, 61, 96, 125, 162, 166, 189, 224, 228, 253, 317, 352, 381, 408, 429; Ted Williams: pp. 154, 156, 167, 178, 182, 184; Jonathan Wright: pp. 110, 111, 113.

Photography Credits:

Contents: iii: Bob & Clara Calhoun/Bruce Coleman, Inc. iv: inset, Bob Winsett/Corbis; FPG. v: Richard Megna/Fundamental Photographs. vi: ESA/Science Photo Library. vii: Roger Werth/Woodfin Camp & Associates, Inc. viii: Gregory Ochocki/Photo Researchers, Inc. ix: Walter Bibikow/FPG.

National Geographic Invitation to Science: S2: Emory Kristof; inset, Harriet Ballard. S3: t. Woods Hole Oceanographic Institution; b. Jonathan Blair.

Be a Scientist: S5: David Mager. S6: NASA. S7: t. Corbis; b, Francois Gohier/Photo Researchers, Inc. S8: l, Jonathan Blair/Woodfin Camp & Associates; r, Wards SCI/Science Source/Photo Researchers, Inc. S11: NASA. S12: John Sanford/Science Photo Library/Photo Researchers, Inc. S13: t, b, NASA. S14: Michael Marten/Science Photo Library/Photo Researchers, Inc. S15: Peter Beck/The Stock Market. S16: l, K. Preuss/The Image Works; r, Richard A. Cooke III/Tony Stone Images S17: Jean Miele/The Stock Market.

Unit 1: 1: Dieter & Mary Plage/Bruce Coleman, Inc.; Randy Morse/Animals Animals, inset b.r. 2: Richard Nowitz/FPG. 3: Ken Karp. 5: Ken Karp, t.r.; R. Calentine/Visuals Unlimited, b. 6: Barry L. Runk/Grant Heilman, b.l.; Runk/Schoenberger/Grant Heilman, b.r. 7: Ken Karp. 8: Sullivan & Rogers/Bruce Coleman, Inc., t.r.; Tom J. Ulrich/Visuals Unlimited, b.c. 9: Cart Roessler/Animals Animals. 10: Ronald H. Cohn. H. S. Terrence 11: Animals Animals. 13: Ken Karp. 15: Ken Karp. 17: C. Bradley Simmons/Bruce Coleman, Inc., t.r.; Jerry Cooke/Animals Animals, b. 18: Jim Zipp/Photo Researchers, Inc., c.; Kim Taylor/Bruce Coleman, Inc., r.; Lefever/Grushow/Grant Heilman, l. 19: Arthur Tilley/FPG. 20: Ken Lucas/Visuals Unlimited, l. 20–21: Skip Moody/Dembinsky Photo Assoc. 21: The Blake School, t. 22: Tim Davis/Zipp/Photo Researchers, Inc. 23: Ken Karp. 24: Dwight R. Kuhn, t.l.; Glenn M. Oliver/Visuals Unlimited, t.c.; Pat Lynch/Zipp/Photo Researchers, Inc., t.r.; Robert P. Carr/Bruce Coleman, Inc., b.l. 25: John Mielcarek/Dembinsky Photo Assoc., b.l.; Nuridsany et Perennou/Zipp/Photo Researchers, Inc. t.l.; Robert L. Dunne/Bruce Coleman, Inc., t.r.; Sharon Cummings/Dembinsky Photo Assoc., b.r.. 26: Henry Ausloos/Animals Animals. 28: Debra P. Hershkowitz/Bruce Coleman, Inc., t.l.; Ken Karp, b.r. 29: Rhoda Sidney/PhotoEdit. 30: Bill Banaszewski/Visuals Unlimited, inset. 30–31: J.C. Carton/Bruce Coleman, Inc., bkgrd. 32: Toyohiro Yamada/FPG. 33: Ken Karp. 34: Inga Spence/Visuals Unlimited, t.c.; Patti Murray/Animals Animals, l. 36: George F. Mobley, l. 37: Bill Bachman/Photo Researchers, Inc. 38: D. Cavagnaro/Visuals Unlimited, t.l.; Dwight R. Kuhn, b.r.; Dwight R. Kuhn, b.l.; John Lemker/Animals Animals, b.c.. 39: Larry Lefever/Grant Heilman. 40–41: Randy Green/FPG, bkgrd.; Stan Osolinski/Dembinsky Photo Assoc. inset t.;. Larry West/FPG, inset b. 41: John M. Roberts/The Stock Market, inset t.; J. H. Robinson/Photo Researchers, Inc., inset b. 43: Superstock; Peter Cade/Tony Stone Images, inset b.r.

44: PhotoDisc., all. 45: Ken Karp. 46: Rob Gage/FPG. 47: Joe McDonald/Animals Animals, b.r.; John Shaw/Bruce Coleman, Inc., t.r. 48: Leonard Rue III/Visuals Unlimited, b.; Robert P. Carr/Bruce Coleman, Inc., t.l. 49: F.C. Millington-TCL/Masterfile, b.r.; Tom McHugh/Photo Researchers, Inc., t.r. 51: Bonnie Kamin/PhotoEdit. 52: Joyce Photographics/Photo Researchers, Inc., t.; Sonya Jacobs/The Stock Market, l. 53: John D. Cunningham/Visuals Unlimited, r.; John Sohlden/Visuals Unlimited, b.l.; Michael T. Stubben/Visuals Unlimited, t.c.; R.J. Erwin/Photo Researchers, Inc., t.l. 54: Ken Karp. 55: Margaret Oechsli/Fundamental Photographs. 56: Dwight R. Kuhn, t.l.; Ken Karp, b.r. 59: Dennis MacDonald/PhotoEdit. 60: Phillip Hayson/Photo Researchers, Inc.

Unit 2: 65: ZEFA Stock Imagery, Inc. 66: Anderson Monkmeyer, b.l.; Dollarhide/Monkmeyer, b.r. 67: Ken Karp, b.r.; Will Hart/PhotoEdit, t.r.. 69: Ken Karp. 70: Barbara Leslie/FPG, b.r.; K.H. Switak/Photo Researchers, Inc., b.l. 71: K. & K. Amman/Bruce Coleman, Inc./PNI. 73: Jacob Taposchaner/FPG. 74: Dan McCoy/Rainbow/PNI. 75: David Young-Wolff/PhotoEdit. 76: Ken Karp. 77: Ken Karp. 78: Ken Karp. 80: RubberBall Productions. 84: Ken Karp. 86: Ken Karp. 87: Ken Karp. 90: NASA. 91: Ken Karp. 92: Ken Karp. 93: Jade Albert/FPG. 94–95: Stephen J. Shaluta, Jr./Dembinsky Photo Assoc. 95: Ken Karp. 97: Chris Salvo/FPG. 98: Camelot/Photonica, b.r.; Jacob Taposchaner/FPG, b.l.; Will & Deni McIntyre/Photo Researchers, Inc., t.c. 99: Ken Karp. 100: Camelot/Photonica, b.l.; Ken Karp, t.l. & m.l. 101: Ken Karp. 103: R. Hutchings/PhotoEdit. 104–105: Ed Degginger/Bruce Coleman, Inc., bkgrd. 105: Jeff Foott/Bruce Coleman, Inc. b. inset; Jonathan Nourok/PhotoEdit, t. inset. 106: Ken Karp. 107: Ken Karp. 109: Ken Karp. 110: Ken Karp, t. & b. 112: Ken Karp. 114–115: The Granger Collection New York. 116: Carl Purcell/Photo Researchers, Inc. 117: Ken Karp. 118: Dollarhide/Monkmeyer. 119: W. Metzen/Bruce Coleman, Inc. 123: Ken Karp. 124: David Mager.

Unit 3: 129: Bkgrd: MMSD Joe Sohm/ChromoSohm. 130: Ken Karp. 131: Ken Karp. inset 132: PhotoDisc. 133: MMSD, m.r.; PhotoDisc, m.c., b.l. & b.r.; Sylvain Grandadam/Photo Researchers, Inc., t.r. 134: Stockbyte. 135: PhotoDisc, b.l.; Ken Karp, t.r. 138: Robert Rathe/NIST; inset, Joe Sohm/Stock, Boston/PNI. 140: Gerry Ellis/ENP Images. 141: Ken Karp. 142: PhotoDisc. 143: PhotoDisc, b.c. & b.r.; Ken Karp, b.l. 144: Lawrence Migdale, l. & b.m.; Margerin Studio/FPG, t.r. 145: Ken Karp. 146: Peter Scoones-TCL/Masterfile. 147: PhotoDisc. 148: Ken Karp. 149: Arthur Tilley/FPG. 150: McGraw Hill School Division. 150–151: Ken Karp, insets. 152: Ken Karp. 153: Ken Karp. 154: Leonard Lessin/Peter Arnold, Inc. 155: PhotoDisc, t.r.; Ken Karp, b.r. 156: Telegraph Colour Library/FPG. 157: Ken Karp. 158: PhotoDisc. 160: Stan Osolinski/Dembinsky Photo Assoc. Charles D. Winters/Photo Researchers, Inc.161: t. Mehau Kulyk/Photo Researchers, Inc. b. William Waterfall/The Stock Market. 163: Eric Meola/The Image Bank; Tom Bean, inset b.r. 164: Ken Karp. 165: Ken Karp. 168: Ben Simmons/The Stock Market, l.; Eric Gay/AP/World Wide Photos, b.r. 169: Ken Karp. 170: Nakita Ovsyanikov/Masterfile, b.r.; Robert P. Carr/Bruce Coleman, Inc., l. 171: Ken Karp. 172: Culver Pictures, Inc. 172–173: Gary Buss FPG, bkgrd. 174: Ken Karp. 175: Ken Karp. 176: Ron Thomas. 177: Gary Withey/Bruce Coleman, Inc., b.r.; Jerome Wexler/Photo Researchers, Inc., t.r.; Ken Karp, b.l.; Telegraph Colour Library/FPG, b.c. 179: Tim Davis/Photo Researchers, Inc. 180: Frank Krahmer/Bruce Coleman, Inc., b.l. 181: Telegraph Colour Library/FPG, bkgrd.; Ken Karp, inset. 183: Ken Karp. 188: PhotoDisc bkgrd.; Ken Karp, insets.

Unit 4: 193: NASA/FPG; inset, GSO Images/The Image Bank. 194: George D. Lepp/Photo Researchers, Inc. 195: Ken Karp. 197: Jim Cummins. FPG. 200: Ken Karp. 201: Andy Levin/Photo Researchers, Inc. 202: Michael R. Whelan, inset; Jim Ballard/AllStock/PNI, t. 204–205: Edward R. Degginger/Bruce Coleman, Inc. 205: Ken Karp. 206–207: John Sanford/Science Photo Researchers, Inc. 208–209: NASA. 210: NASA, b.l.; Michael P. Gadomski/Photo Researchers, Inc., t.l. 211: Richard T. Nowitz/Corbis. 212: Chris Dube. 212–213: t. Photo Disc. 213: The Granger Collection New York. 214: Matt Bradley/Bruce Coleman, Inc. 215: Ken Karp. 217: Archive Photos/PNI, b.r.; Ken Karp, b.l. 218: Frank Rossotto/The Stock Market. 219: Rev. Ronald Royer/Photo Researchers, Inc. 220–221: Pekka/Photo Researchers, Inc. 222-223: Visuals Unlimited. 225: Science Photo Library/Photo Researchers, Inc. 226: Mike Yamashita/Woodfin Camp & Associates. 227: Ken Karp. 228: Jerry Schad/Photo Researchers, Inc. 229: Francois Gohier/Photo Researchers, Inc., b.; Jerry Lodriguss/Photo Researchers, Inc., t. 231: Detlev Van/Photo Researchers, Inc., t.; Ken Karp, b. 232: Jim Cummins/FPG. 233: t. NASA/Photo Researchers, Inc. b. Telegraph

R47

Colour Library/FPG 234: Palomar Observatory/Caltech. 235: Ken Karp. 238: NASA/Mark Marten/Photo Researchers, Inc., b.; US Geological/Photo Researchers, Inc., t. 239: NASA/Science Source/Photo Researchers, Inc., b.; US Geological Survey/Photo Researchers, Inc., t. 240: Ken Karp. 241: Mugshots/The Stock Market. 242: A. Ramey Stock Boston, l. NASA/JPL/Corbis; 242–243: USGS/Photo Researchers, Inc., bkgrd. 243: NASA/Corbis, b.r. Photo Researchers, Inc., bkgrd. 245: Ken Karp. 246: Science Photo Library/Photo Researchers, Inc. 247: Ken Karp. 248: NASA, t.; NASA/Mark Marten/Photo Researchers, Inc., b. 249: NASA Science Photo Library/Photo Researchers, Inc., b.; Space Telescope/Photo Researchers, Inc., t. 250–251: Jerry Lodriguss/Photo Researchers, Inc. 251: Nieto/Jerrican/Photo Researchers, Inc. 252: Sam Zarembar/The Image Bank, bkgrd.; The Granger Collection, inset.

Unit 5: 257: ZEFA/Stock Imagery, Inc. 258: PhotoDisc, b.l.; Ann Purcell/Photo Researchers, Inc., b.r.; Jeffrey Myers/FPG., t.r. 259: Ken Karp. 260: Joyce Photographics/Photo Researchers, Inc., b.c.; Ken Karp, t.l., m.l., b.l., b.r. 261: Ken Karp. 262: PhotoDisc, bkgrd; Ken Karp, insets. 263: l. col. from top, Stephen Ogilvy, Ken Karp, Stephen Ogilvy, E.R. Degginger/Photo Researchers, Inc.; r. col. from top, Stephen Ogilvy, Ken Karp, Ken Karp, Charles R. Belinky/Photo Researchers, Inc. 264: Diane Rawson; Photo Researchers, Inc., b.l.; Josef Beck/FPG, m.l.; Tim Davis/Photo Researchers, Inc, b.r. 265: Yann Arthus-Bertrand/Corbis. 266: Art Wolfe/AllStock/PNI, t.; Robert Harding Picture Library, inset; 267: Fergus O'Brien/FPG International, t.; D. E. Cox/Tony Stone Images, m. 268: Francois Gohier/Photo Researchers, Inc. 269: Ken Karp. 270: Keith Kent/Science/Photo Researchers, Inc., bkgrd.; Susan Rayfield/Photo Researchers, Inc., inset l & r. 271: Ken Karp. 272: Farrell Grehan/Photo Researchers, Inc., t.; Ken M. Johns/Photo Researchers, Inc., b. 273: Ken Karp. 274: Dan Guravich/Photo Researchers, Inc. 275: Ralph N. Barrett/Bruce Coleman, Inc. 276: Adam Jones/Photo Researchers, Inc., t.r.; John Sohlden/Visuals Unlimited, b.r.; W. E. Ruth/Bruce Coleman, Inc., b.l. 276–277: PhotoDisc., bkgrd. 277: The National Archives/Corbis, t.r.; Pat Armstrong/Visuals Unlimited, b.l.; Sylvan H. Wittaver/Visuals Unlimited, t.l. 278: Warren Faidley/International Stock. 279: Ken Karp. 280: NASA/GSFC/Photo Researchers, Inc. 281: PhotoDisc. 282: Paul Sakuma/AP/Wide World Photos, b.; Will & Deni McIntyre/Photo Researchers, Inc., t. 283: PhotoDisc. 284: Arthur Rothstein/AP Photo, b.; Sergio Dorantes, t. 285: The Weather Channel. 286: Jeffrey Howe/Visuals Unlimited. 286–287: Telegraph Colour Library/FPG, bkgrd. 287: Frank Rossotto/The Stock Market, t.r.; NOAA/Science Photo Library/Photo Researchers, Inc., m.r.; Dr. Denise M. Stephenson-Hawk, b.r. 289: PhotoDisc, bkgrd.; Stock Imagery, Inc., inset. 290: PhotoDisc, b.r.; Michael P. Gadomski/Photo Researchers, Inc., b.l.; Peter Skinner/Photo Researchers, Inc., t.r. 291: Ken Karp. 292: Craig K. Lorenz/Photo Researchers, Inc. 294: Ken Karp. 295: Ken Karp. 296: Jim Foster/The Stock Market, b.; M. E. Warren/Photo Researchers, Inc., t. 297: Debra P. Hershkowitz/Bruce Coleman, Inc. 298: The National Archives/Corbis, inset. 298–299: John Elk III/Bruce Coleman, Inc., bkgrd. 299: G. Buttner/Okapia/Photo Researchers, Inc., b.r.; Roy Morsch/The Stock Market, t.r. 300: Liaison Agency, b.r.; Owen Franken/Corbis., b.l. 301: Ken Karp. 302: Phillip Hayson/Photo Researchers, Inc., t.; Richard Hamilton Smith/Corbis., b. 303: Ray Ellis/Photo Researchers, Inc. 304: Will McIntyre/Photo Researchers, Inc. 305: Ken Karp. 306: Bruce Byers/FPG, b.c.; Ken Karp, t.b.l. 306–307: Jeffrey Sylvester/FPG. 307: Norman Owen Tomalin/Bruce Coleman, Inc., r. & b.;Steve Kline/Bruce Coleman, Inc., inset. 308: Lawson Wood/Corbis. 309: Ken Karp. 310: PhotoDisc. 311: Ken Karp. 312: PhotoDisc. b.l. Stuart Cahill/AFP/BETTMAN. 315: PhotoDisc. 316: David Sucsy/FPG bkgrd.; Barbara Comnes, inset.

Unit 6: 321: Craig K. Lorenz/Photo Researchers, Inc., bkgrd; Richard Price/FPG, inset. 322: Renee Lynn/Photo Researchers, Inc. 323: Ken Karp. 324: Gary Randall/FPG, b.; Lee Foster/Bruce Coleman, Inc., t. 329: Jon Feingersh/The Stock Market. 330: George F. Mobley, t.; 1998 Comstock, Inc., inset. 331: Emory Kristof. 332: Tim Davis/Photo Researchers, Inc. 333: Ken Karp. 334: Gary Meszaros/Visuals Unlimited. 336: Farrell Grehan/Photo Researchers, Inc., r. ; Rod Planck/Photo Researchers, Inc., l. 337: Ken Karp. 340-341: clockwise from top: Charles Gold/The Stock Market; Denise Cupen/Bruce Coleman, Inc.; Roy Morsch/The Stock Market. Don Mason/The Stock Market; Ed Bock/The Stock Market; Elaine Twichell/Dembinsky Photo Assoc.; J. Barry O'Rourke/The Stock Market; J Sapinsky/The Stock Market; Rex A. Butcher/Bruce Coleman, Inc. 340–341: Telegraph Colour/FPG. 342: Ken Karp. 343: Ken Karp. 345: Dennie Cody/FPG, l; DiMaggio/Kalish/The Stock Market, r. 346: Paul A. Zahl, l; William E. Townsend/Photo Researchers, Inc., r. 347: Arthur Norris/Visuals Unlimited, l.; Biophoto Associates/Photo Researchers, Inc., r. 348: Ken Karp, b.; Zig Leszcynski/Animals Animals, t. 349: Lynwood Chase/Photo Researchers, Inc. 353: Gil Lopez-Espina/Visuals Unlimited, inset; K & K Ammann/Bruce Coleman, Inc., bkgrd. 354: Michael Gadomski/Photo Researchers, Inc. 355: Ken Karp. 356: Joe McDonald/Bruce Coleman, Inc., t.; John Shaw/Bruce Coleman, Inc., b. 358: Ken Karp. 359: Kenneth W. Fink/Bruce Coleman, Inc. 361: Ken Lucas/Visuals Unlimited. 362: Richard Kolar/Animals Animals, l.; Richard & Susan Day/Animals Animals, b. 363: Ken Karp. 365: Barbara Gerlach/Visuals Unlimited, t.; Zefa Germany/The Stock Market, b. 366: A. Cosmos Blank/Photo Researchers, Inc., b.l.; Breck P. Kent/Animals Animals, t.; Robert P. Carr/Bruce Coleman, Inc., b.r. 367: Ken Karp. 369: Emily Stong/Visuals Unlimited. 370: Art Wolfe/Tony Stone Images t.c.; Tom Brakefield/The Stock Market, b. 371: Gerald & Buff Corsi/Visuals Unlimited, t.l.; Stephen Dalton/Photo Researchers, Inc., t.r.; Dan Suzio/Photo Researchers, Inc., b. 372: David Weintraub/Photo Researchers, Inc. 373: Ken Karp. 374: Keith Gunnar/Bruce Coleman, Inc., l.; Phil Degginger/Bruce Coleman, Inc., r. 375: Pat & Tom Leeson/Photo Researchers, Inc. 376: Joe McDonald/Visuals Unlimited. 377: Joe & Carol McDonald/Visuals Unlimited. 378: Ken Karp., b., Omikron/Photo Researchers, Inc., t. 379: Pat & Tom Leeson/Photo Researchers, Inc. 380: Photo Disc t.; Janis Burger/Bruce Coleman, Inc., t.r.; Jen and Des Bartlett/Bruce Coleman, Inc., b.l.; Tom Van Sant/The Stock Market, bkgrd.

Unit 7: 385: George Schiavone/The Stock Market. 386: Gary Landsman/The Stock Market. 387: Ken Karp. 388: Yoav Levy/Phototake. 389: Barbara Peacock/FPG. 392: Ken Karp. 393: Ken Karp. 394: Michael Townsend/Tony Stone Images, t.; Randy Taylor/Liaison Agency, inset; 395: Bob Daemmrich/The Image Works. 396: David Waldorf/FPG. 397: Ken Karp. 399: David M. Phillips/Visuals Unlimited. 401: Manfred Kage/Peter Arnold, Inc. 402: Ken Karp. 403: Mary Kate Denny/PhotoEdit. 404: CORBIS/BETTMANN–UPI. 405: Sandy Fox/MMSD. 406: Howard Sochurek/The Stock Market, inset; Deborah Gilbert/The Image Bank, b. 407: Telegraph Colour Library/FPG, bkgrd. r. McGraw Hill School Division. 409: Otto Rogge/The Stock Market; t. Tracy/FPG. 410: Joyce Photographics/Photo Researchers, Inc., l.; Steven Needham/Envision, r. 411: Ken Karp. 412–413: Ken Karp. 414: David Young-Wolff/PhotoEdit, t.; Ken Karp, b. 417: Michael Newman/PhotoEdit. 418: NASA/Photri, b.r. & m.r. 419: NASA/Photri, t.r., m.r. & b.r.; NASA/Corbis, inset top. 418–419: Ronald Royer/Photo Researchers, Inc. 420: David Young-Wolff/PhotoEdit. 421: Ken Karp. 422: Michael A. Keller/The Stock Market. 426: Ken Karp. 428: Bkgrd: PhotoDisc.

Handbook: Steven Ogilvy: pp. R6, R8, R12, R14, R15, R26.